Matthew Ritchie

Matthew Ritchie
Proposition Player

Lynn M. Herbert

With essays by
Laura Steward Heon
Jenelle Porter

Interview with the artist by
Thyrza Nichols Goodeve

Contemporary Arts Museum Houston in association with Hatje Cantz Publishers

LEFT: INSTALLATION VIEW, *MATTHEW RITCHIE: PROPOSITION PLAYER*, CONTEMPORARY ARTS MUSEUM HOUSTON, 2003

Lenders to the Exhibition

c/o Atle Gerhardsen, Berlin
Dimitris Daskalopoulos Collection, Greece
The Fabric Workshop and Museum, Philadelphia
John Kaldor, Sydney, Australia
Ninah and Michael Lynne
Mass MoCA
Private Collection, New York
Matthew Ritchie
Andrea Rosen Gallery, New York
Allison and Neil Rubler
Phil Schrager Collection, Omaha
John A. Smith and Vicky Hughes

This catalogue has been published to accompany the exhibition *Matthew Ritchie: Proposition Player* organized by Lynn M. Herbert, Senior Curator, for the Contemporary Arts Museum Houston, December 12, 2003 – March 14, 2004.

Matthew Ritchie: Proposition Player has been made possible by a grant from the National Endowment for the Arts, a federal agency, and by the patrons, benefactors, and donors to the Museum's Major Exhibitions Fund:

NATIONAL
ENDOWMENT
FOR THE ARTS

MAJOR PATRON
  Fayez Sarofim & Co
PATRONS
  Eddie and Chinhui Allen
  Mrs. Nancy C. Allen
  Mr. and Mrs. A. L. Ballard
  Mr. and Mrs. I.H. Kempner III
  Ms. Louisa Stude Sarofim
  Mr. and Mrs. Michael Zilkha
BENEFACTORS
  Robert J. Card, M.D./Karol Kreymer
  George and Mary Josephine Hamman Foundation
  Rob and Louise Jamail
  Susan Vaughan Foundation
DONORS
  Baker Botts L.L.P.
  James A. Elkins, Jr.
  KPMG LLP
  Jeanne and Michael Klein
  Lester Marks
  Karen and Eric Pulaski
  David and Suzanne Saperstein
  Jeff Shankman
  Leigh and Reggie Smith
  Stephen and Ellen Susman
  Mr. and Mrs. Wallace S. Wilson

The exhibition catalogue is supported by The Brown Foundation, Inc.

Table of Contents

Marti Mayo, Director

Foreword and Acknowledgements

Over the five decades since its founding in 1948, the Contemporary Arts Museum Houston has organized exhibitions that bring the best of the new and the now, of art that is not yet history, to a broad audience. Some of the Museum's visitors are knowledgeable about contemporary art and theory; some are much less familiar with the art we show and study. But all have benefited from the numerous important one-person exhibitions presented here. In its first fifteen years, the Museum mounted exhibitions of the work of international figures such as Alexander Calder, Max Ernst, Lyonel Feininger (the Museum's first one-person show), Amedeo Modigliani, Pablo Picasso, Rufino Tamayo, and Vincent Van Gogh—all of whose work was seen as revolutionary at the time. After its second decade, as art moved beyond easel-sized canvases and sculpture "on a pedestal," and the Museum began presenting shows by such major new artists such as Robert Rauschenberg and Mark Rothko, the decision was made to construct a building that would be more hospitable to monumental work and art made from nontraditional materials. Gunnar Birkerts's striking stainless-steel building, completed and opened in 1972, was designed to showcase this challenging new art.

Even Birkerts, however, probably did not anticipate how welcoming today's Brown Foundation Gallery would be to the artists who would use its immense parallelogram-shaped space as inspiration for the rich variety of site-specific installations seen by our audiences over the last thirty years. Recent examples of large-scale exhibitions planned specifically for the gallery include *Richard Long: Circles, Cycles, Mud, Stones* (1996); *Ann Hamilton: kaph* (1999); and the present project, *Matthew Ritchie: Proposition Player*. With equal doses of intelligence and magic, Ritchie has transformed this space into an exploration of ideas about the universe, ideas that intersect with art history and criticism, mathematics, philosophy, literature, physics, and a number of other disciplines. With vision and wide-ranging knowledge, Ritchie has combined a variety of media, some incorporating new technology, others embracing traditional art materials, to pose fascinating and provocative questions.

Matthew Ritchie: Proposition Player has been made possible by a grant from the National Endowment for the Arts, a Federal agency, Washington, D.C., and the prescient individuals, foundations, and corporations who are contributors to the Museum's Major Exhibition Fund: Major Patron—Fayez Sarofim & Company; Patrons—Eddie and Chinhui Allen, Mrs. Nancy C. Allen, Mr. and Mrs. A. L. Ballard, Mr. and Mrs. I. H. Kempner III, Ms. Louisa Stude Sarofim, and Mr. and Mrs. Michael Zilkha; Benefactors—Robert J. Card/Karol Kreymer, the Hamman Foundation, Rob and Louise Jamail, and the Susan Vaughan Foundation; Donors—Baker Botts LLP, James A. Elkins Jr., KPMG LLP, Jeanne and Michael Klein, Lester Marks, Karen and Eric Pulaski, David and Suzanne Saperstein, Jeff Shankman, Leigh and Reggie Smith, Stephen and Ellen Susman, and Mr. and Mrs. Wallace S. Wilson. The Fund supports projects presented in the Brown Foundation Gallery, and on behalf of the audiences we serve, we thank these civic-minded donors who have provided the resources that allowed us to present this project at a level the art deserves. All museum publications in the 2003–2004 season are supported by a generous grant from The Brown Foundation Inc., allowing us to document the scholarship surrounding museum-originated exhibitions and to preserve temporary projects for the study and enjoyment of audiences beyond Houston.

Museum operations are supported by the Cultural Arts Council of Houston/Harris County, by the Houston Endowment Inc., and by the Museum's members, patrons, and donors whose support and attention means so much to all of us.

The project has been organized by Senior Curator Lynn M. Herbert, who has worked directly with the artist over several years to bring it to fruition. Her unique combination of knowledge, experience, skill, imagination, and willingness to work coopera-tively with the artist and others has produced a rewarding project for us all. She has contributed as well an insightful and illuminating essay to this catalogue. Ms. Herbert has been a longtime member of the Museum's curatorial staff and guides its work with sensitivity and expertise. Ritchie's project is only the most recent example of her many substantial contributions to our program, and the board, staff, and audiences of the Museum are grateful for her dedication and vision.

No exhibition is mounted without considerable assistance from outside the institution. Ms. Herbert wishes to especially thank Andrea Rosen and Sarah Cohen of the Andrea Rosen Gallery, New York, who have provided invaluable assistance and support throughout the project's organization. Steven Sergiovanni, a former associate of the gallery, was also helpful in the early stages of the exhibition's planning. She is also grateful to Atle Gerhardsen and Sabine Schmidt of c/o Atle Gerhardsen Gallery, Berlin, for help in Europe. Jess Frost and Jordan Bastien, assistants to Matthew Ritchie, were also instrumental in the project's realization.

The catalogue has been imaginatively and sensitively designed by Conny Purtill with the assistance of Jenelle Porter, who has also contributed an essay to the publication that captures both the spirit and essence of the tales within Ritchie's work. Laura Heon, Curator, MassMOCA, North Adams, Massachusetts (where the exhibition will be presented in a slightly different form later in 2004), has written an important contribution tracking the evolution of Ritchie's aesthetics. Thyrza Nichols Goodeve's interview with the artist adds to our understanding of his thought processes and working methods. Victoria Kin has researched and contributed the materials for the artist's biography, bibliography, and other documentation on his career. Early assistance with this documentation was provided by Museum intern Mavis Kelsey III. This publication has been ably edited by Polly Koch. We are grateful to our co-publisher, Hatje Cantz, and particularly to its Director of International Sales, Markus Hartmann, for his efforts on the Museum's behalf.

An important contribution to the exhibition was made by a Spring 2003 workshop led by artist Karyn Olivier at Wharton Elementary School of the Houston Independent School District. We thank Dr. Bob Sandburn, Executive Director of the Education Foundation of Harris County, and Monica Sandoval, Principal, Wharton Elementary School, for assisting with the organization of the workshop. The following students from Wharton participated in the project: Denise Aguilar, Brandon Boyd, Tish Condado, Doren Garcia, Nora Garcia, Oscar Gonzalez, Brenda Gonzalez, Jeremy King, Natalia Lopez, Martin Milan, and Vinh Ngo.

As a noncollecting institution focused on temporary exhibitions, the Contemporary Arts Museum Houston is dependent on the generosity and good will of the lenders of works of art. This project is no exception and we are indebted to those listed on page 6 who have agreed to part with their works so that others may enjoy them.

To produce and install an exhibition of the scale and ambition of *Matthew Ritchie: Proposition Player* requires considerable effort and dedication on the part of the Museum's staff. Almost all members of the staff played some role in the realization of the project and we are grateful for this help. Ms. Herbert wishes to particularly recognize the following for assistance above and beyond their required duties: Registrar Tim Barkley for oversight of the loans and their transportation as well as thought and care during the installation; Preparator Jeff Shore for planning assistance and accomplishing the especially complicated and demanding installation; Paula Newton, Director of Education, and Peter Precourt, Teen Council Coordinator, for efforts with the Wharton Elementary School Workshop and other special and regular programming; and Ellen Efsic, Director of Development, for procuring needed resources.

Finally, all of us—the Museum's board and staff as well as the audiences who will benefit from the exhibition—owe a debt of gratitude to the artist. Matthew Ritchie is an extraordinary individual who operates from a position of continuous openhandedness. A stimulating collaborator and cooperative partner, he infused the project with enthusiasm, good will, and energy. His work, his wide-ranging intellect, and his generosity of spirit have made the project a wonderful and rich learning experience.

FIG. 1: *COFFIN WEATHER* (DETAILS), 2003. VINYL ON WALL (INSTALLED ON FACADE OF THE CONTEMPORARY ARTS MUSEUM HOUSTON). 88 x 288 INCHES (223.52 x 731.52 CM). COURTESY THE ARTIST, ANDREA ROSEN GALLERY, NEW YORK, AND MASS MOCA

Catalogue of the Exhibition

All works are courtesy the artist and Andrea Rosen Gallery, New York, unless otherwise indicated. Dimensions are listed height preceding width preceding depth.

After Lives, 2002
Oil and marker on canvas
88 x 154 inches (224 x 391 cm)
COLLECTION ALLISON AND NEIL RUBLER

The Big Life, 2002
Oil and marker on canvas
88 x 154 inches (223 x 391 cm)
COLLECTION JOHN KALDOR, SYDNEY,
AUSTRALIA

The Eighth Sea, 2002
Oil and marker on canvas
99 x 121 inches (251 x 307 cm)
COLLECTION THE ARTIST

We Are Folded, 2002
Oil and marker on canvas
88 x 121 inches (224 x 307 cm)
DIMITRIS DASKALOPOULOS COLLECTION,
GREECE

Coffin Weather, 2003
Vinyl on wall
88 x 288 inches (225 x 732 cm)
COURTESY THE ARTIST AND MASS MOCA

The Fine Constant, 2003
Powdercoated aluminum, steel,
gypsum, wax, and enamel
95 x 1,152 x 192 inches
(241 x 2926 x 488 cm)

The First Sea, 2003
Oil and marker on canvas
99 x 110 inches (251 x 279 cm)
PHIL SCHRAGER COLLECTION, OMAHA

Five of a Kind, 2003
suite of five framed drawings
The Function Suite
The Box Factory
The Anti City
The New Place
The Slow Tide
Graphite and ink on Denril
14 x 44 inches each (34 x 528 cm)
COLLECTION THE ARTIST

Giant Time, 2003
Oil and marker on canvas
99 x 132 inches (251 x 335 cm)
PRIVATE COLLECTION, NEW YORK

*A Glorious Martyrdom Awaits Us
All at the Hands of Our Tender
and Merciful God*, 2003
Oil and marker on canvas
88 x 99 inches (224 x 251 cm)
COURTESY THE ARTIST, ANDREA ROSEN
GALLERY, NEW YORK, AND C/O ATLE
GERHARDSEN, BERLIN

The God Impersonator, 2003
Matthew Ritchie in collaboration with
The Fabric Workshop and Museum,
Philadelphia
Rubber, adhesive, and Tyvek
$1/4$ x 288 x 576 inches
(.64 x 732 x 1,463 cm)
COURTESY THE ARTIST, WITH THE FABRIC
WORKSHOP AND MUSEUM, PHILADELPHIA,
AND ANDREA ROSEN GALLERY, NEW YORK

The Hierarchy Problem, 2003
Acrylic on wall
12 x 139 feet (3.6 x 42.3 m)
Edition of 1 with one AP

Proposition Player, 2003
Powdercoated aluminum,
Minicel foam, rubber, adhesive,
electronic components,
one pair cast resin dice, and custom
designed deck of cards
42 x 42 x 98 inches
(107 x 107 x 249 cm)
Edition of 1 with one AP

A Glorious Martyrdom Awaits Us

Self-Portrait in 2064, 2003
Oil and marker on canvas
80 x 100 inches (203 x 254 cm)
COLLECTION NINAH AND MICHAEL LYNNE

Snake Eyes, 2003
Oil and marker on canvas
99 x 132 inches (251 x 335 cm)

The Two-Way Joint, 2003
Photographic print on Duratrans,
aluminum frame, and fluorescent light
96 x 192 x 2 inches
(244 x 488 x 6 cm)

Where I'm Coming From, 2003
Oil and marker on canvas
99 x 121 inches (251 x 307 cm)
COLLECTION JOHN A. SMITH AND VICKY
HUGHES

FOLLOWING PAGES: INSTALLATION VIEWS, *MATTHEW RITCHIE: PROPOSITION PLAYER*, CONTEMPORARY ARTS MUSEUM HOUSTON, 2003

Lynn M. Herbert

Knight of Infinity, Champion of Enlightenment

Most people live in worldly sorrow and joy, and sit around the walls and they don't join in the dance. But the Knights of Infinity are dancers and possess elevation. They rise up and fall and this is no mean pastime, nor ungraceful to behold.

From *Fear and Trembling* (1843), Soren Kierkegaard[1]

At game time, Matthew Ritchie showed up on the field with an array of discarded college textbooks, forty-nine fictional characters taken from history, science, mythology, and assorted religions, an outmoded palette of colors, and an inordinate amount of energy. It was an inauspicious beginning, to say the least. Yet he stood his ground and set out to create a map of everything—a map of everything from the Big Bang up to the present. The crowd was bemused and skeptical. Who was this artist, declaring under the harsh glare of the contemporary art world's stadium lights that he, that *he*, was going to create a body of work that encapsulated a history of the universe? And with such hopelessly outdated equipment, no less. Needless to say, the money wasn't on Ritchie's succeeding, but you had to admire the young fellow's gumption, so we stayed and we watched. And were we ever richly rewarded.

All the world loves an underdog, and when against all odds, the underdogs start winning, we love them all the more. Their success and their victory invigorate us and somehow become our own. When an Everyman beats the odds, it's as if we can't get enough of it. Ritchie's secret weapon, it turned out, was energy: the energy fueling the insatiable curiosity with which he set off on his quest, the energy he used to harness and give structure to the range of forces that his map describes, and the energy that formally revealed itself in the work's telling. All of these energies have combined to create a work that is at once exhilarating, exuberant, expansive, effusive, enchanting, and exquisite. [Note: All are words beginning with the letter "e"—in Ritchie's multilayered and multidimensional lattice of a cosmology, you quickly learn to be ever alert and receptive to such seeming coincidences as one might be a link to the underlying structure of the universe, to the essential

1. In *Fear and Trembling*, the Danish philosopher Kierkegaard uses the Biblical tale of Abraham's willingness to sacrifice his son to promote the idea that a man can have an exceptional mission in life. Such men, Kierkegaard's "Knights of Infinity," are the people among us who, while outwardly normal in appearance, inwardly possess a great courage, passion, energy, and faith. This quote was sent to Matthew Ritchie by his mother, Carole Ritchie, on October 22, 2003.

interrelatedness of all things, to the world's "implicate order."][2]

But first, back to that young artist. Having attended art school in London in the 1980s, Ritchie found himself, in 1995, working as a building superintendent in Manhattan, taking care of a building near New York University. At the end of each semester, students would throw away textbooks they didn't want to keep, and Ritchie began collecting books on a wide array of subjects. After extensive reading, the artist, a model autodidact, emerged from his basement studio invigorated and intoxicated with "the pure pleasure of thought" and "the exhilaration of connecting with knowledge."[3]

"I wouldn't call myself a scholar," Ritchie explains, "but I did as much research as an ordinary person who's a building superintendent can manage in his spare time—into the history of color, into competing religious systems in the West and their relationship to philosophical and political structures, how those in turn were related to the evolution of early scientific practices, and how that evolved into contemporary scientific practice. I looked at things like high-temperature physics and biology and the relationships between them that collectively form what we would like to believe is an objective truth about the nature of our lives. All that was cooking away in my brain, and then bizarrely enough, I decided to try and force it into the brightly colored waistcoat of contemporary painting."[4]

Ritchie's intoxication was fueled by the "implicate order" he found in our seemingly chaotic universe. Advances in computer technology were fueling a staggering number of developments in contemporary science. Beautiful truths were revealing themselves left and right, and for Ritchie, the possibilities seemed endless. Many would have looked to other artists who sought to express greater truths through their paintings. Mark Rothko (1903–1970), Barnett Newman (1905–1970), Kazimir Malevich (1878–1935) and Piet Mondrian (1872–1944) all pursued a kind of intangible absolute or truth. All chose to follow a reductive route, approaching their subject by paring things down and limiting their vocabulary of forms and palette to a minimum. Ritchie, however, an enthusiastic member of the information saturation age, was unwilling to relinquish the details and chose instead to search for a way to share as much of this information as possible. He looked, instead, to the likes of William of Ockham, a fourteenth-century scholar and Franciscan monk. A kindred polymath, Ockham weighed in on an impressive range of topics, including the theory of knowledge,

logic, ethics, theology, and political philosophy. He was a great assimilator and today is best remembered for the principle "Ockham's razor," which advises that no more assumptions should be made than are necessary. More importantly to Ritchie, Ockham was a pioneering champion of the individual's human and intellectual rights and the responsibilities that accompany those rights at a time when such notions were almost unheard of.

People born under the sign of Aquarius are notorious for being grand visionaries and unfettered dreamers. Ritchie, who was born under the sign of Capricorn, explains with his innately dry wit that Capricorns are Aquarians with Palm Pilots. Fortunately, Ritchie was born with organizational skills up to the challenge of keeping pace with his far-reaching intellect and boundless imagination. He's not the first of his peers to have sought to incorporate great quantities of information within their work. One thinks of such Hanne Darboven installations as her epic *Kulturgeschichte* 1880–1983 [*Cultural History* 1880–1983], (1980–83, fig. 2) composed of 1,590 sheets of 27 1/2 x 19 3/4 inches and nineteen sculptural objects, which archives a time period by incorporating personal documents as well as cultural, social, and historical memorabilia. The individual elements are arranged in loose categories but are not subordinated to a particular narrative or underlying structure. Rather, as art historian Lynne Cooke has noted, Darboven "seems to surrender to its excess."[5] Her sheets of information, hung almost floor to ceiling in a close-knit grid formation that wholly fills a large gallery, invite, as Cooke notes, "not a reading but a visual experience."[6] Similar in presentation and equally panoramic is Gerhard Richter's ongoing *Atlas* (begun in 1964), a vast framed archive of approximately 4,000 images including snapshots, sketches, postcards, and clippings from magazines that have served as a kind of database or "atlas" of memories and visual inspiration for the artist.

Matt Mullican's project of creating a kind of reductive, almost clinical pictographic dictionary of the world comes a step closer to Ritchie's work in that Mullican has chosen to organize his material into five categories and assigned each a specific color. Mullican's "five divisions of the universe" are as follows: "Yellow: The World Framed (art world); Green: the elemental World (nature); Blue: the World Unframed (mundane objects that fill our world); Black and White: The World of Languages and Signs (rational network of information and definitions); and Red: The Subjective World (as

2. In his book *Wholeness and the Implicate Order* (London: Routledge, 1980), the eminent theoretical physicist David Bohm (1917–1992) promoted the term "implicate order" in his efforts to understand the world as comprising multiple levels of interconnectedness from the subatomic realm on up.
3. Matthew Ritchie, quoted in Jeffrey Kastner, "An Adventurer's Map to a World of Information," *The New York Times*, October 15, 2000, p. 37.
4. Ibid.
5. Lynne Cooke, "Hanne Darboven," online posting, 1995, Dia Center for the Arts, New York, <http://www.diacenter.org/exhibs_b/darboven/essay.html>.
6. Ibid.

FIG. 2: HANNE DARBOVEN, *KULTURGESCHICHTE 1880–1983 (CULTURAL HISTORY 1880–1983),* 1980–83. FROM INSTALLATION AT DIA CENTER FOR THE ARTS, 548 WEST 22ND STREET, NEW YORK CITY. 3/28/96–6/29/97

close to spirituality as he gets)."[7] The symbolic use of color appears in Ritchie's work as well, but Ritchie eschews the lexicographic mode of working in favor of organizing his information in the form of a narrative—a grand continuum of tales. As such, his work invites both a visual experience and a reading. The scope of Ritchie's project, his drive, and his chosen approach to his subject as a teller of tales is similar in many respects to that of the great epic poets, Dante Alighieri (1265–1321) and John Milton (1608–1674), and the twentieth-century novelist and short story writer Italo Calvino (1923–1985).

Like Ritchie, Dante was a voracious reader and seeker of knowledge, but gaining access to information was much more difficult during the Middle Ages. As historian Archibald T. MacAllister has noted: "The young explorer from medieval Christendom went doggedly on from one work to another which he had seen mentioned, without adequate teachers, courses, reference works, or indeed the works themselves, except as he could beg or borrow the manuscripts."[8] Dante shared Ritchie's democratic inclinations and the desire to provide all of his information to his fellow man. Toward that end, Dante took the unusual step of publishing the *Commedia [The Divine Comedy]* (1308), not in Latin, but instead in the humble Tuscan vernacular so that the common man could read his tale. Dante's story takes the reader on a journey through Hell (*Inferno*), then Purgatory (*Purgatorio*), and finally to Paradise (*Paradiso*) in a process that allegorically explores one man's journey to God, including the notion of free will and the resulting rewards and punishments. Like Ritchie, Dante's intent was to uplift his audience. He was convinced that "love was the most important force behind noble actions and lofty endeavors" and with his journey to paradise through many of the horrors and injustices of his own day, Dante wanted "to remove those living from the state of misery and lead them to the state of felicity."[9]

In telling a tale that encompasses the entire universe, Dante found structure to be his salvation just as it would become Ritchie's centuries later.[10] Dante's tale is told in the first person with Dante narrating as both an everyman and himself, a thirteenth-century poet from Florence. Everyman-Dante embarks on his journey accompanied by Virgil, the epic poet of ancient Rome, who represents human reason. Maps and charts of the different realms Dante and Virgil travel through are often published alongside the text of the *Commedia* as an aid to the reader, outlining specific locations and their inhabitants. Diagrams have similarly proven helpful to those wanting a map of the events unfolding in a given Ritchie work (pp. 94–95). In Dante's "Eighth Circle of Hell" (fig. 3), we find just below a waterfall a sequence of cavities housing such ne'er-do-wells as Panderers and Seducers, Flatterers, Simonists (sellers of ecclesiastic favors and offices), Sorcerers, Barrators, Hypocrites, Thieves, Deceivers, Sowers of Discord, and Falsifiers. Such a provocative grouping is in keeping with some of the characters to be found in Ritchie's tales, many of whom were also culled from the underbelly of society (for an engaging introduction to Ritchie's cast of characters and a synopsis of his tale, see Jenelle Porter's "Five Percent More," p. 96).

Ritchie's tale, on the other hand, is told in the third person. Centered on the world of science, it emanates structurally from an overall chart, *The Working Model*, (1997, p. 116) composed of forty-nine elements or characters that are divided into seven groups of seven. In addition to representing a specific character, each element also represents a specific physics attribute and property. As Ritchie explains: "It's a cast of fragments, a model of multiple schizophrenia, or playfulness and catastrophe. The personalities of the freaks reflect their flawed natures. Each of the 'characters' represents a single, narrow-minded commodity like light or volume. Only by combining can they form any kind of functioning whole. It was important for me that there be no winners, no dominant group or sexual dynamic, no hero or central narrative. Everybody is a player."[11] Ritchie's initial seven characters, "The Watchers," correspond to the seven regions of the brain and are also identified as the "gang of seven celestial agents [who] have been thrown out of heaven." The next seven characters, who actually represent earlier earth events, are the "Gamblers," corresponding to the building blocks of the universe. In one story, "The Fast Set," a lost astronaut, a lonely actress, a broken Golem, and an awakened child come together in a love triangle that also represents a particular law of thermodynamics. And on it goes.

In John Milton's *Paradise Lost* (1674), we find a magnitude and baroque sensibility that bring us still closer to Ritchie. As a polymath, Milton is considered by many to be unparalleled: his reading lists show his interests to have been wide-ranging and his linguistic abilities to have embraced at least ten different languages.[12]

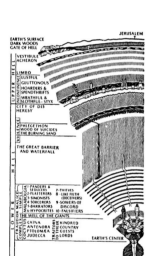

EARTH'S SURFACE / DARK WOODS / GATE OF HELL / JERUSALEM

FIG. 3: "ILLUSTRATION" BY C.W. SCOTT-GILES, COPYRIGHT © 1984 BY MARK MUSA, FROM *THE DIVINE COMEDY* BY DANTE, TRANSLATED BY MARK MUSA. USED BY PERMISSION OF PENGUIN, A DIVISION OF PENGUIN GROUP (USA) INC.

7. Holland Cotter, "Matt Mullican: Public Paradise," in *Matt Mullican: Banners, Monuments, and the City as an Exhibition of Work for Public Spaces* (Philadelphia: Moore College of Art and Design, get year) <http://www.thegalleriesatmoore.org/publications/mullicanhc.shtml>.

8. Archibald T. MacAllister, "Introduction," in *The Inferno*, by Dante Alighieri, translated by John Ciardi (New York: Penguin Putnam Inc., 1982) p. xx.

9. Mark Musa, "Introduction," in *The Portable Dante*, by Dante Alighieri, (New York: Penguin Books, 1995), p. xxx.

10. MacAllister, p. xxiv. MacAllister explains: "In our utilitarian scorn we are in danger of forgetting that a certain preoccupation with form (and even today's straight line betrays such a preoccupation) is essential to beauty. In the *Divine Comedy* we must remember that Dante had for his subject the whole world, the entire universe, all of man's history, his learning, his beliefs, plus his own particular messages. To him preoccupation with form was not extrinsic, not a luxury; it was his salvation. As Mr. Gilbert Highet points out, is this that sets Dante apart from his contemporaries, this was the great lesson he learned from his master and author, Virgil."

11. Matthew Ritchie, quoted in Patricia Ellis, "Matthew Ritchie: That Sweet Voodoo That You Do," *Flash Art*, November/December 2000, p. 91.

12. Roy Flannagan, *John Milton: A Short Introduction* (Oxford: Blackwell Publishing Company, 2002), p. 10. Flannagan notes: "... there is no one that I know of, living or dead, who has read all the books that we know Milton read in his lifetime. The man was a phenomenal linguist, comfortable in French, Italian, Spanish, Latin, Greek, at least knowledgeable about Hebrew, Arabic, Syriac, Aramaic, and what was known as Chaldaic."

[Ritchie attended St. Paul's School, the same parochial school in London that Milton did]. In *Paradise Lost*, Milton brought all of this knowledge to bear on a tale that on the surface describes the battles between heaven and hell, and the fall of Adam and Eve, but underneath fairly seethes with all manner of philosophical, political, religious, literary, and scientific learning. In Milton's epic we find a uniquely visual and dynamic style of writing that lends itself to comparison with other arts. As Milton scholar Roy Flannagan describes it: "Milton's epic swirls from heaven to hell to earth, and it swirls backwards and forwards in time. The baroque is sometimes defined as art barely within control, or art at the boundaries of existence. The energy of *Paradise Lost* is incessantly moving (in both senses of the word), as in the famous oxymoron 'darkness visible,' with a restless energy. . . . And his images carry a baroque energy as surely as do the images of a Rubens or a Rembrandt. Probably the closest pictorial parallel to *Paradise Lost*, to go back one generation to Michelangelo, is in the end-panel of the Sistine Chapel, the image of Christ in Judgement, with hell and heaven spread out above his head and below his feet."[13] (More on Michelangelo later). The amplitude and intensity of all of the spiraling and swirling about in *Paradise Lost*, the clashing of one force against another, and the jumping backward and forward in time in the story is in keeping with Ritchie's own modus operandi. Fittingly, Ritchie's cast of forty-nine characters includes Mulciber, a fallen angel who in *Paradise Lost* is the architect of Satan's headquarters, Pandaemonium. He is considered to be an archetype of all artists, including the epic poets, as well as alluding to the artist and architect, Bernini (more on Bernini later, too).

To move yet another step closer to understanding Ritchie's strategy, it is also helpful to look at the work of Italo Calvino. Calvino was a member of Oulipo (*Ouvroir de Littérature Potentielle* or the Workshop of Potential Literature), a group of writers, historians, and mathematicians interested in creating a kind of metafiction by subjecting their writing to various mathematical rules and word games. One such exercise was Georges Perec's lipogrammatic novel *La Disparation [A Void]* (1969), which was written without ever using the letter "e"—no small feat as "e" is the most frequently used letter in the French language.[14] As you may have noticed, Ritchie has devised a letter game of his own for this catalogue: the four letters used to denote the four constants of the universe—

e, h, G, and c (the electron charge, the Planck limit, gravity, and the speed of light)—have been printed in the colors that correspond to the four suits in the *Proposition Player* deck of cards (pp. 57–63).

Calvino, like Ritchie, was a fantasist who found himself drawn to the narrative possibilities and inherent contradictions lurking in the ever evolving realm of science. In his group of short stories, *Cosmicomics* (1965), each story is introduced with a scientific finding and followed by a story based on that finding, as told from the point of view of Calvino's narrator, Qfwfq (whose name is a palindrome). For instance, in "Games Without End," Calvino introduces the Steady State Theory, a theory of the universe's origin in opposition to the Big Bang theory. He follows it with Qfwfq's tale of how during his childhood, he and his sometime friend, the "incorrigible cheat" PfwfP, engaged in a spirited game of marbles using hydrogen atoms that escalated into a game of "flying galaxies" once they hurled all of their atoms into the sky. As Qfwfq tells it: ". . . I took all of the new atoms I was hiding and flung them into space. At first they seemed to scatter, then they thickened together into a kind of light cloud, and the cloud swelled and swelled, and inside it some incandescent condensations were formed, and they whirled and whirled and at a certain point became a spiral of constellations never seen before, a spiral that poised, opening in a gust, then sped away as I held on to its tail and ran after it."[15] For years, Ritchie himself has written narratives that nimbly transform scientific abstracts into more earthbound human dramas (pp. 102–114). These texts, like Calvino's, often begin with the scientific basis for what is going on (and in Ritchie's case, how he has formally presented it), and then go on to bring the science alive by telling a tale that gives it a human dimension.[16]

For *The Castle of Crossed Destinies* (1969), Calvino set up an entirely different game. A group of travelers overnighting at a castle discover, while seated around a table together, that they have lost their ability to speak. Each then has to relate his own personal story utilizing a shared deck of tarot cards (fig. 4). Calvino explained: "This book is made first of pictures—the tarot playing cards—and secondly of written words. Through the sequence of the pictures the stories are told, which the written word tries to reconstruct and interpret."[17] Calvino's use of tarot cards allowed him to conjure up a seemingly infinite number of intertwining tales, much as Ritchie has been able to do with his forty-nine original characters, each of

13. Ibid, pp. 74–75.

14. A lipogram is a text in which one or more letters are not allowed to appear.

15. Italo Calvino, "Games Without End," in *Cosmicomics* (New York: Harcourt Brace & Company, 1968), pp. 66–67.

16. Alan P. Lightman, an astrophysicist who has written several best-selling novels that engage science, including *Einstein's Dreams* (1993), acknowledges the influence of Calvino. It is interesting to note the slow but steady increase in the number of books written by scientists that humanize what they do, bringing the seemingly inexplicable into the realm of the known, in effect broadening the boundaries of Magic Realism in literature. For more on this subject, see Emily Eakin, "Art and Science Meet with Novel Results," *The New York Times*, October 18, 2003, pp. 17 and 19.

17. Italo Calvino, "Note," in *The Castle of Crossed Destinies* (Orlando, Florida: Harcourt, Brace & Company, 1976), p. 123. Calvino goes on to explain (p. 126): "I publish this book to be free of it: it has obsessed me for years. I began by trying to line up tarots at random, to see if I could read a story in them. 'The Waverer's Tale' emerged; I started writing it down; I looked for other combinations of the same cards; I realized the tarots were a machine for constructing stories; I thought of a book, and I imagined its frame: the mute narrators, the forest, the inn; I was tempted by the diabolical idea of conjuring up all the stories that could be contained in a tarot deck."

FIG. 4: ILLUSTRATION FROM ITALO CALVINO, "THE CASTLE OF CROSSED DESTINIES," IN *TAROT'S: THE VISCONTI PACK IN BERGAMO AND NEW YORK* (MILAN: FRANCO MARIA RICCI EDITORE, 1969)

FOLLOWING PAGES: *THE GOD IMPERSONATOR*, 2003. MATTHEW RITCHIE IN COLLABORATION WITH THE FABRIC WORKSHOP AND MUSEUM, PHILADELPHIA. RUBBER, ADHESIVE, AND TYVEK. 1/4 × 288 × 576 INCHES (.64 × 732 × 1,463 CM). COURTESY THE ARTIST, THE FABRIC WORKSHOP AND MUSEUM, PHILADELPHIA, AND ANDREA ROSEN GALLERY, NEW YORK.

whom, like a tarot card, represents certain attributes. Indeed, for *Proposition Player* Ritchie has made a deck of playing cards (pp. 57–63) incorporating his own forty-nine characters and further has linked specific poker hands to specific paintings (p. 64). Such gestures are a tip of the hat to Calvino as well as an homage to the game that his own project has become.[18]

We wouldn't be talking about the resolve and strategies behind Ritchie's work if the work itself didn't capture our attention, intrigue us, and compel us to want to know more. Just how has Ritchie taken these epic and open-ended literary structures and given them physical and visual form? Michelangelo Buonarroti (1475–1564) faced a similar dilemma when he received a papal commission to paint the twelve Apostles in the spandrels between the arches leading up to the Sistine Chapel ceiling. As with Ritchie's work, Michelangelo's project grew, in his case to encompass a representation of the world before Moses. For such a monumental task, Michelangelo embedded each scene into its own space within the architecture, utilizing the entire barrel of the 134-foot long vaulted ceiling, the vault compartments above the windows, the lunettes around the windows, and the spandrels (fig. 5). Ritchie, too, has used the architectural surroundings of his site-specific installations to organize the individual scenes of his narrative, allowing them to interact in varying combinations. *Proposition Player* is Ritchie's largest-scale effort to date, and like the Sistine Ceiling, it creates an entire environment that cannot be taken in with a single glance, but rather invites walking in and around and perusing. However, while a sixteenth-century viewer could, to some extent, "read" or "know" the stories portrayed in Michelangelo's epic installation, Ritchie's tales remain more abstract and elusive to his twenty-first-century viewers.

In the spirit of all things being interconnected, Dante, Milton, and Michelangelo would centuries later inspire the author, illustrator, and bookseller William Blake (1757–1827). Blake studied the musculature of Michelangelo's figures through engravings and transferred their strength into his own illustrations for an 1808 edition of Milton's *Paradise Lost*. Having revered Milton since childhood, Blake wrote of his own "great ambition to know everything."[19] In addition to illustrating the writings of others (including Dante's *Commedia* which he worked on up until his death in 1827), the well-read Blake also published and illustrated his own prophetic writings.

These brought together his thoughts about the politics, religion, and science of the day as seen through the characters of a mythological system entirely his own and driven by his lifelong worship of "energy" of a more spiritual nature.[20] Like Ritchie's, Blake's characters were drawn together from a variety of sources, but unlike Ritchie's, his tales exalt the realm of the spiritual over that of science. Yet Blake's characters, such as Albion, the Ancient Man (fig. 6), the false prophet Urizen ("Your Reason"), and Los, a stand-in for the artist and imagination (Los appears as the Golem in Ritchie's story, "The Fast Set," [2000]), convey the same sense of urgency and fundamental importance that Ritchie's characters do, and they share an ethereal, otherworldly quality with the anthropomorphic characters found in Ritchie's digital animations and drawings on vellum (pp. 28–37). Further, a critic writing about Blake's work could just as well have been considering Ritchie's when he wrote: "In Blake's art, figures are flat and lined up as if in a frieze; forms swirl, swim and fly by, but in a shallow space. Color carries much of the expressive baggage. He was an exquisite colorist."[21]

Coming forward in time, Joseph Beuys, Sigmar Polke, and Robert Rauschenberg are three contemporary artists that Ritchie himself credits with having been particularly influential during his own formative years. Beuys was a standard bearer for incorporating everything that one is interested in into one's work, no matter how disparate those interests might be. Politics, folklore, alchemy, and history could all come together in a single work and in a meaningful way, be it in a performance, a sculpture, an installation, or whatever media Beuys deemed appropriate. For Ritchie, Beuys brought back and legitimized the role of content in art, and Polke showed what could happen when Beuys' blend of formal and intellectual freedom entered into the realm of painting. Similarly, Ritchie recalls Rauschenberg's 1958–60 suite of drawings illustrating Dante's *Inferno* as being particularly influential. Through them he recognized Rauschenberg not only as the last of the classicists, but as a notably inclusive one, embracing all manner of imagery from all manner of sources. No closed mythology, Rauschenberg's suite of illustrations includes solvent transfers from newspapers, comics, and magazines, and his Dante and Virgil are represented by characters as diverse as contemporary politicians, athletes, and astronauts (a classic modern-day archetypal hero, an astronaut named "Dynamis" appears in Ritchie's story, "The Fast Set" [2000]). Ritchie

FIG. 5: MICHELANGELO (1475–1564). GENERAL VIEW OF THE SISTINE CEILING, SISTINE CHAPEL, VATICAN PALACE

FIG. 6: WILLIAM BLAKE (1757–1827). *GLAD DAY, OR THE DANCE OF ALBION*, c. 1794. SINGLE COLOR PRINT. 10 1/2 x 7 3/4 INCHES (27 X 20 CM). BRITISH MUSEUM, LONDON

18. Further, the suite of five drawings created for the exhibition, "Five of a Kind" (2003), pp. 28–37, directly refer to Ritchie's cards with each of the five drawings corresponding to one of the five levels of Ritchie's game explained in his "Rules" (p. 57).
19. Peter Ackroyd, *Blake* (London: Minerva, 1996), p. 56.
20. Peter Quennell, *A History of English Literature* (Springfield, Mass.: Merriam Company, 1973), p. 247. It is also interesting to note that Ritchie, too, has had a hand in book illustration, illustrating Ben Marcus' *The Father Costume* (Sebastapol, Calif.: Artspace Books, 2002).
21. Michael Kimmelman, "A Visionary Whose Odd Images Still Burn Bright," *The New York Times*, March 30, 2001, p. B31.

admired Rauschenberg's "open consciousness, spatially and in time," and his ability to bring a feeling of exciting visual contemporanaeity to the centuries-old tale.[22]

The energy and enthusiasm with which Ritchie embraced this inclusive spirit is present in the work itself. Nothing is ever at a standstill in Ritchie's realm—everything is always moving and unfolding, endlessly changing, growing, birthing, evolving, and morphing. In keeping with the baroque nature of his tales, his works have the same spinning, swirling, gravity-defying feeling and movement to be found in the works of such great seventeenth-century masters as Gian Lorenzo Bernini (1598–1680). A sculptor, painter, and architect like Michelangelo, Bernini was a master of drama and stagecraft, be it in the awe-inspiring colonnades of his piazza at St. Peter's in Rome (1656–67) or the mushrooming spectacle that is his *Cathedra Petri* (1657–66, fig. 7). Ritchie, who has breathed life into his personifications of figures from religion and mythology and activated his spaces just as Bernini did, ups the ante still more through his incorporation of science. Conceptually and visually, Ritchie's works pull us right into the domain of quantum mechanics—the subatomic realm where even "empty space is not empty, but rather foaming with energy."[23] Centrifugal forces meet stretching forces meet explosive forces meet entropy. The site-specific allover wall drawings suggestive of scientific notations have a manic, self-generating, and ever-expanding urgency. It is as if we are in the presence of a moment of eureka when the brain is spilling out revelations faster than the human hand can write. It is the same kind of physical and rhythmic energy we feel when standing before a work by Jackson Pollock (1912–1956), the allover drip painting with its highly charged lattices of splattered paint obscuring the hidden pictographs lurking below.

And if paint or ink, canvas or vellum can't keep up with Ritchie's vision, he deftly engages other media. For *Proposition Player*, the artist has created *The Fine Constant* (2003), a large-scale sculpture that brings drawing off the wall and into the viewer's space (pp. 2, 13–15, 50–51) and *The God Impersonator* (2003), a mosaic of rubber tile that allows viewers to literally walk into his work (pp. 20–21). He has utilized lenticular technology to create *The Two-Way Joint* (2003), a stained-glass-like image that changes as one walks around it (pp. 26–27), and digital technology to create *Proposition Player* (2003), an animated gaming table with digital

dice (pp. 52–54). He has even breathed new life into the age-old template of playing cards by assigning a character from his own cosmology to each card leaving it up to us to decide whether to play a friendly game of blackjack or to venture into a more richly metaphorical world akin to tarot, Pokemon, or Yu-Gi-Oh (pp. 57–63).[24]

All of Ritchie's works are infused with a generous use of color. No chromophobe, Ritchie wholly embraces color: "All the big technological civilizations were gaudy, the Greeks and Romans painted the hell out of those elegant white statues and temples, the Victorians just painted everything, and even the Sistine Chapel has been restored to its original Technicolor print."[25] From the get go, Ritchie assigned each of his forty-nine characters a color, creating a systematized palette that alluded to each character's qualities and attributes metaphorically. Collectively, it resembles a retro 1970s palette, populated by avocados, sunset golds, and rich burgundies. His early stylized and flat use of color has evolved into a richer palette, with modeling and articulation steadily gaining ground on stylization. Ever one to cheat on his system to make a painting better, Ritchie has allowed his palette and style of painting to evolve with his story.

With *Proposition Player*, Ritchie finds himself well into the infinite continuum that is his tale, with a seemingly endless number of possible intersections and interactions before him (à la Calvino's infinite tarot combinations). His system of characters, attributes, and colors has advanced to the point of becoming a kind of artificial intelligence—a primal self-generating force capable of taking him, if he so chooses, on an endless number of adventures.

Ritchie's engaging way of exploring our universe and his imaginative way of bringing so many different kinds of ideas together will always leave us wanting to know more, wanting to know the story behind each individual work—which cataclysmic events are unfolding, which scientific principles are being enacted, which battles are being fought or won, and who the ever-colorful and insightful players are at any given moment. No matter how generous a raconteur Ritchie is, with his own written narratives as well as shared accounts in interviews, we will always want more. That underdog who boldly announced that he was going to make a map of everything has in fact beaten the odds—he's dazzled us. We won't ever understand every bit of what's going on at every level in his work, any more than we can in Milton's *Paradise Lost*, Dante's

22. Matthew Ritchie, a conversation with the author, August 27, 2003.
23. Dennis Overbye, "The End of Everything: The Universe Might Last Forever, Astronomers Say, But Life and Intelligence Might Not," *The New York Times*, January 1, 2002, p. D7.
24. Ritchie acknowledges the United States Government's "52 Most Wanted Iraqis" card deck produced at the time of the 2002 Iraq invasion as a source of inspiration, albeit ironic, for his own deck of cards (conversation with the author, August 27, 2003).
25. Ellis, p. 91.

FIG. 7: GIAN LORENZO BERNINI (1598–1680). *THE CATHEDRA (CHAIR) OF ST. PETER* (1656–67). ST. PETER'S BASILICA, VATICAN STATE

Commedia, or Michelangelo's Sistine Chapel. That frustration is part and parcel of the beauty of it. Artist Ronald Jones wrote of Ritchie's work: "To understand his work as merely abstract is like looking deep into the Rosetta stone without attempting to decipher its hieroglyphic and demonic texts. Ritchie's art is not an enigma, nor is it useful to downgrade it as the self-centered expression of a stable subjectivity; it is the ignition key to amazing legends.… I reflected on what a terrible shame it would have been had we decided to give up on [Lewis] Carroll or [Marcel] Duchamp at the moment they became complex. We should rise up as far as we can to glimpse Ritchie's atlas of the universe, knowing we can only rise so far for now."[26]

All of the exhilarating, exuberant, expansive, effusive, exquisite, and enchanting works that Ritchie has created since he embarked on his ambitious quest have brought a response quite different from that of the first fans watching in the stands. The playful almost euphoric language adopted by so many who have written about these works would suggest that they have been all but swept up into Ritchie's energy-filled continuum:

Mr. Ritchie's work has an almost Mozartian lightness and energy that takes the viewer into a scintillating yet cerebral never-never land where myth and science, gods and atoms pirouette, mingle and metamorphose among swirling clouds interspersed with snaky, death-of-Laocoön coils.[27]

Hypnotic libido rhythms gyrate chemical compound hues; Mandalas of geometric signifiers are altarpieces for bargaining. They combust their big bang enlightenment across the walls, and spill pools of passionate algorithms over the floors. Others are like tribal tattoos, cryptic totems of goblins and ghoulies reenacting the fabled laws of legend.… This is romantic gesture, a love story of tainted tenderness. Some kind of radioactive Rococo spiraling out of control in a passionate surge.[28]

The underdog has dazzled his audience, and with *Proposition Player*, he dazzles us yet again. That initial slit he made in the fabric of our knowing all those years ago has grown wider still, offering us more new ways of seeing and understanding our universe. A museum gallery has been transformed into a laboratory, a chapel,

an atlas, an epic poem … into Ritchie's own "information casino." Ritchie is that proposition player, the independent contractor hired by the casino to invite you to play a friendly game of cards, and as we step in, we find that we can literally roll the dice for the future of the universe. He is our Dante, our guide through this amazing celebration of knowledge. As he surrounds us on all sides, we find ourselves pulled still further into the energy with which Ritchie set about mapping the universe, the energy that enabled him to pull it all together, the energies that he portrays, and the energy with which he presents it. These energies engage us so wholeheartedly that we ourselves are energized in return. This invigoration and heightened sense of awareness is so complete as to feel thrillingly intrinsic. With the beauty of the implicate order laid out before us, it is as if we are suddenly able to revel and delight in everything, from a triumph of good over evil to the trails of our own atoms spinning and swirling about us as we walk, talk, or breathe.

The path of enlightenment is not an easy one. It requires a tremendous amount of resolve and belief in one's cause. Of Milton's decision to try to write *Paradise Lost*, literary scholar Northrup Frye wrote: "To decide to write an epic of this kind is an act of considerable courage, because if one fails, one fails on a colossal scale, and the echo of ridicule may last for centuries."[29] And yet the rewards of such a journey can reach far beyond our imaginations. Fortunately for us, Ritchie, like Milton, chose to take that chance. And in so doing, Ritchie, like Kierkegaard's Knights of Infinity, has found a way to lift us above our worldly sorrow and joy, to possess elevation. With *Proposition Player*, he invites us to join in the knights' dance, and we come to understand the richness of Kierkegaard's words when he wrote: "… this is no mean pastime, nor ungraceful to behold."

26. Ronald Jones, "Continued Investigation of the Relevance of Abstraction," *frieze*, June/July 1999, p. 102.

27. Roberta Smith, "Cracking the Same Mold with Different Results," *The New York Times*, November 15, 2002, p. B36.

28. Ellis, pp. 90–91.

29. Northrop Frye, "The Story of All Things," in *Paradise Lost: An Authoritative Text, Backgrounds, and Sources Criticism*, edited by Scott Elledge (New York: W. W. Norton, 1993), p. 510.

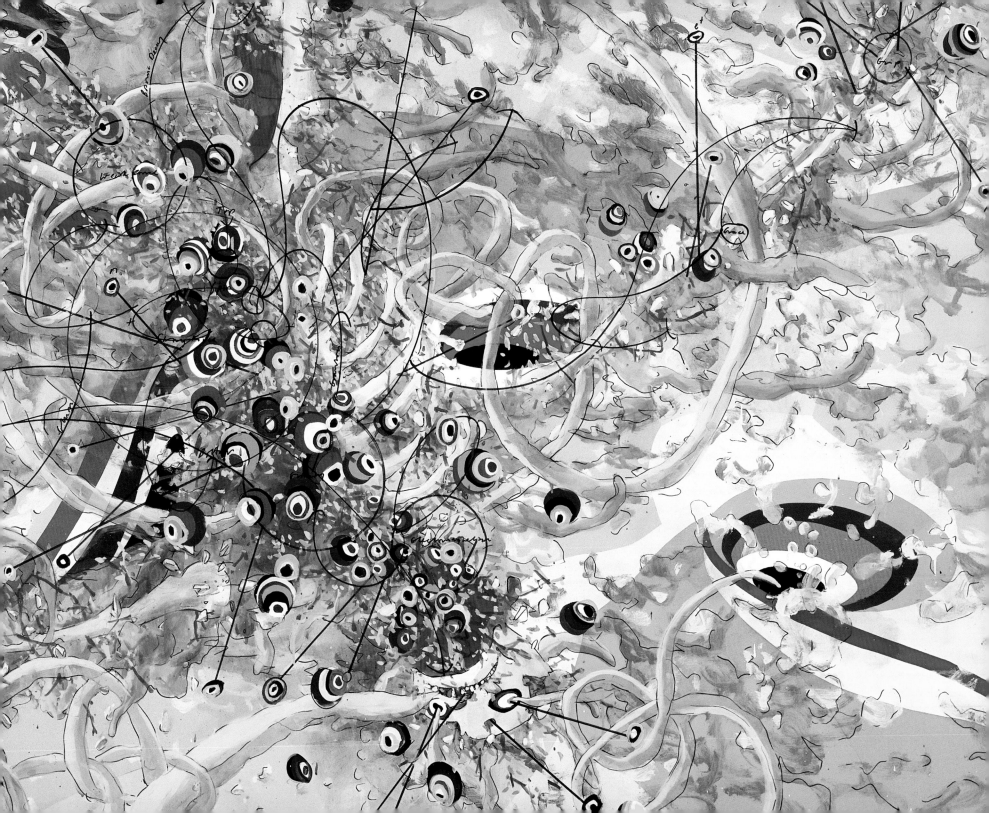

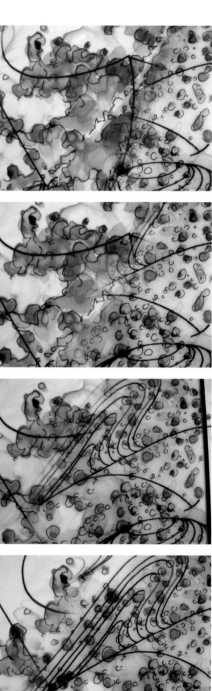

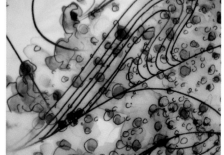

ABOVE: *THE TWO-WAY JOINT* (INSTALLATION VIEW), 2003. PHOTOGRAPHIC PRINT ON DURATRANS, ALUMINUM FRAME, FLUORESCENT LIGHT. 96 x 192 x 2 INCHES (244 x 488 x 6 CM). COURTESY THE ARTIST AND ANDREA ROSEN GALLERY, NEW YORK

RIGHT: DETAILS OF *THE TWO-WAY JOINT*, ILLUSTRATING FROM TOP TO BOTTOM HOW THE IMAGE CHANGES WHEN SEEN FROM DIFFERENT VANTAGE POINTS

BOTTOM LEFT AND OPPOSITE PAGE: *THE TWO-WAY JOINT* (INSTALLATION VIEWS), 2003

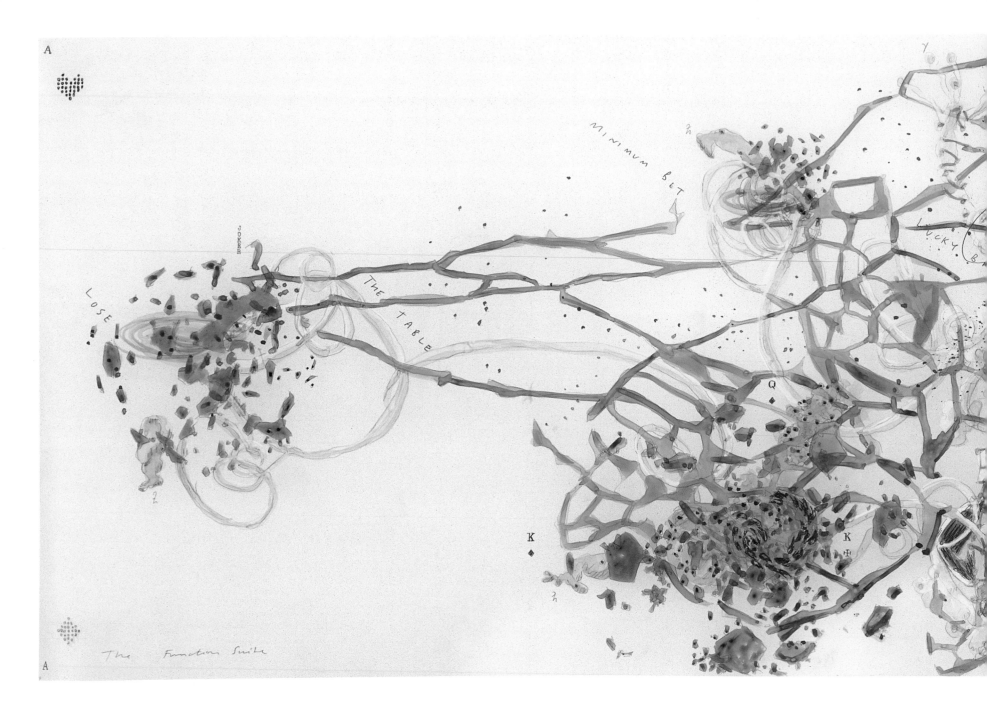

THE FUNCTION SUITE FROM *FIVE OF A KIND*, 2003. GRAPHITE AND INK ON DENRIL. 14 x 44 INCHES (34 x 528 CM). COLLECTION THE ARTIST

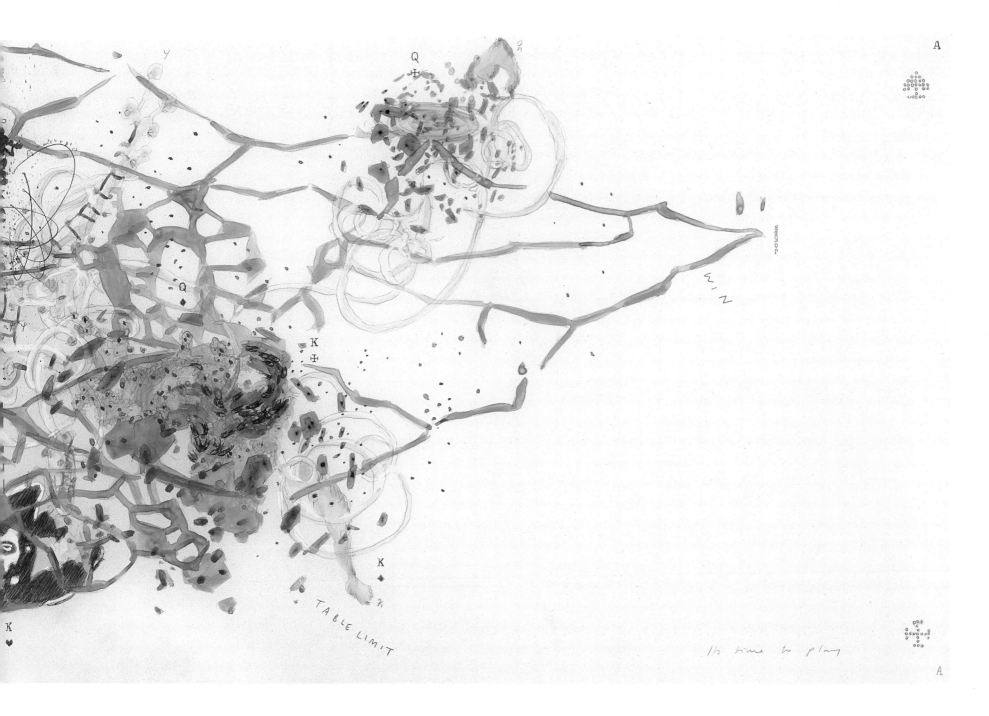

TABLE LIMIT

It's time to play

CRAPS

PLANCK MASS = 5.56 × 10⁻⁵ GRAMS

The Box Factory

THE BOX FACTORY FROM *FIVE OF A KIND*, 2003. GRAPHITE AND INK ON DENRIL. 14 x 44 INCHES (34 x 528 CM). COLLECTION THE ARTIST

The Anti City

THE ANTI CITY FROM *FIVE OF A KIND*, 2003. GRAPHITE AND INK ON DENRIL. 14 x 44 INCHES (34 x 528 CM). COLLECTION THE ARTIST

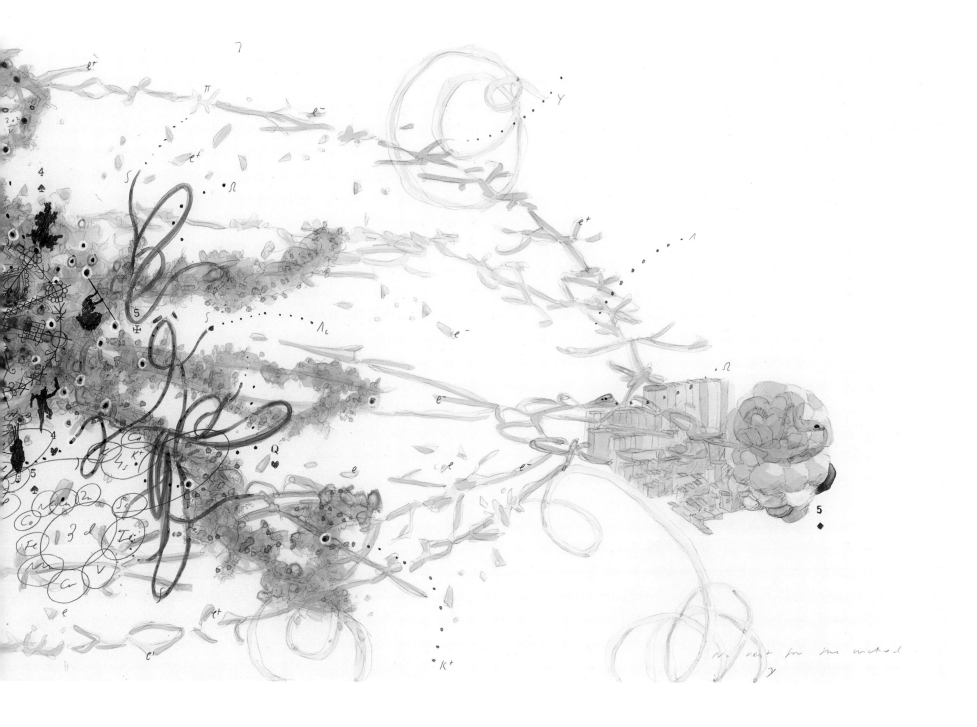

no rest for the wicked

THE NEW PLACE FROM *FIVE OF A KIND,* 2003. GRAPHITE AND INK ON DENRIL. 14 x 44 INCHES (34 x 528 CM). COLLECTION THE ARTIST

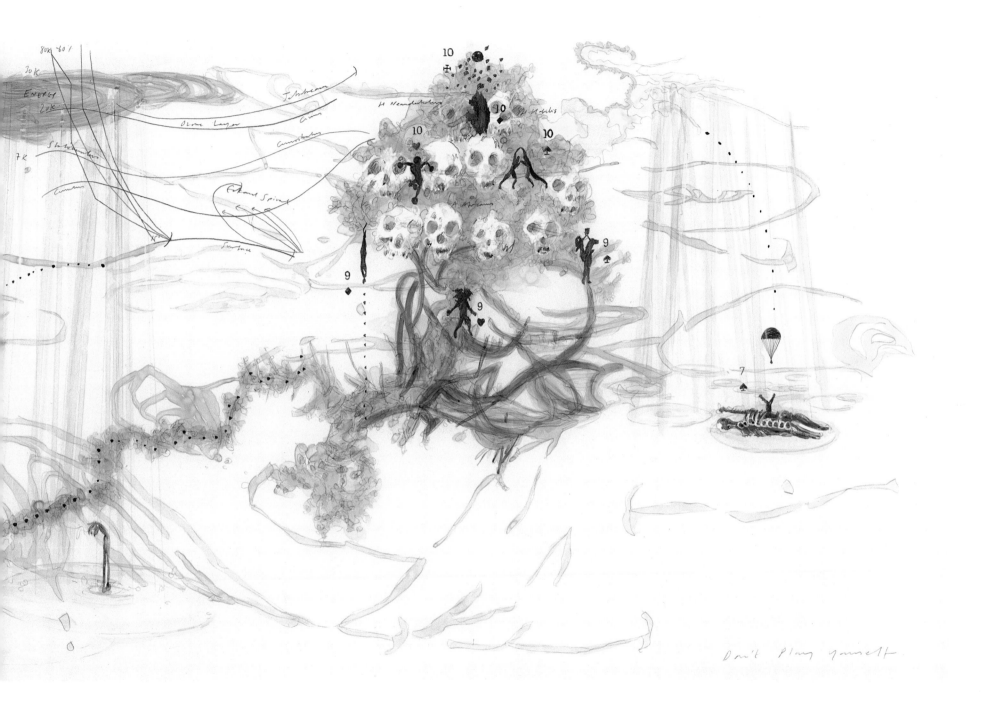

THE SLOW TIDE FROM *FIVE OF A KIND*, 2003. GRAPHITE AND INK ON DENRIL. 14 x 44 INCHES (34 x 528 CM). COLLECTION THE ARTIST

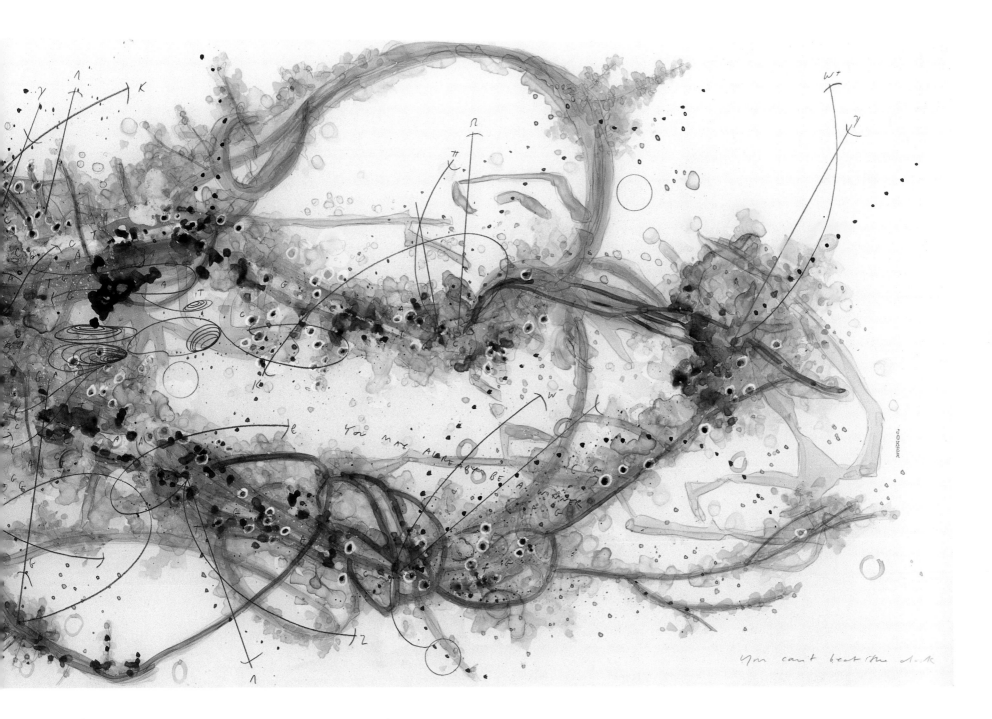

Thyrza Nichols Goodeve

Reflections on an omnivorous visualization system:
An Interview with Matthew Ritchie

I always thought the best magic tricks were the ones you knew how they worked but, the trick was so perfect you still couldn't help believing it. There are seven kinds of magic trick. The disappearance, the production, the transformation, the mentalist demonstration, the anti-scientific demonstration, penetration, and the transportation. Now imagine if one trick did them all at once.

Matthew Ritchie, 2003

TG As the story goes, I'd like to begin with a brief history of the project. How did it begin?

MR In 1995, after many years of working as a building superintendent and not really making art, I got started again by making a list, and then the list turned into a map, and the map turned into a story, and then the story turned into a game. Since then I have typically worked episodically, through a series of site-specific projects that cumulatively described elements of a system or, more accurately, a way of working. I think this accumulation sometimes created the illusion of a progression, with a hierarchy of meaning. But it turns out that impression is even less than half the story. This show is a good time for me to evaluate the truth of that first impression and how closely it is related both to the true intentions of the work and to the physical forms it has taken on over time.

TG What was the initial list?

MR It was a list of everything I was interested in. It was grouped as forty-nine categories arranged in a grid of seven by seven, things like solitude, color, DNA, sex, everything I could think of. Each element on the list was represented in seven ways: as a scientific function, a theological function, a narrative function, a color, a form, a dynamic function, and finally through a personal, hidden meaning. But once they started crossing over from their little boxes, which happened immediately, that's when it turned into a map, like a place, as if all the elements had become little cities one would like to visit. And then it became a story, almost automatically.

TG What was the function of the forty-nine characteristics? I mean, ultimately, what were you trying to get at?

MR The forty-nine characteristics were originally an attempt to simply represent the conditions of any system. Light, color, mass, space, time, etc. are aspects shared by painting with any cosmology or any representation of the universe. The many shows that followed were an exploration of the possibility of building consensus, or form, from contradictory narratives. Cape Canaveral and Morris Lapidus for Miami, the Brockton Holiday Inn and glacier climbing in Svalbard for the shows in [respectively] Boston and Oslo, the geological oddity of the Seven Cities for a show in São Paulo. Each show added physical details to the overall information architecture, trying to extend the idea of an open system to the physical form of the work.

TG The more I've looked at and thought about your work, the more it has become about manifesting structures of information and the information age, not just about painting. Or better, you're using the medium of painting not to represent the issues and ideas of the information age but to translate them into another order, an order that is physical, where, as you put it, everything is there all at once.

MR I want to be able to see everything. It's a fathomless desire, a weakness and a strength. But to do such a thing, you have to turn information into a physical form.

TG Which is so interesting because one of the most dramatic distinctions between the information age and the pre-information age is the increasing invisibility and non-physical form of things, like subway tokens becoming metro cards; coins and paper, credit, and ATMs; film into digital streams, etc.

MR Yes, so we need to make a visual metaphor for all the things we cannot see. I grew up with the information age. When I was in high school a digital watch was a rare trophy. Now a tidal wave of information engulfs us. They have just introduced a unit of measure that calculates planetary information flow. More information was exchanged in the last five years than in all human history. How do we deal with all this? How do we create a meaningful information envi-

1. Matthew Ritchie, quoted in interview by Jennifer Berman, *BOMB* Spring 1997, p. 64.

ronment? How can we learn to see information as form? I've always been interested in this idea of anthropomorphizing information and have wanted to use painting to prove one of the fundamental premises of information theory, that any sufficiently complex system will acquire its own internal meaning. Not only can you see all of it, but it can see all of you. I have also wanted to see if I could introduce certain fixed relationships into painting that would allow it to acquire the status of language. Then maybe this thing could talk back. I don't know much about linguistics, but once I came across a list of the properties of language, and painting has all but one.

TG Which is?

MR Intertranslatability. It fascinated me that painting could be considered mute. In language the word "blue" can be translated into any language and will still always means "blue." But in painting there is no way to translate Picasso's blue or El Greco's blue from painting to painting. Pigments can't be translated: they are specific, never general, never translatable.

TG In 1997, in an interview with Jennifer Berman for *BOMB*, you said, "…there are a lot of artists … who are doing work that I feel close to, and it evolves around ideas of treating art as language, and consequently inventing narratives, but not in some sixties way…."[1] Could you elaborate on that?

MR I guess what I was getting at is any discussion of my personal narrative must be closely linked to the personalized global practices that emerged in 1995–2000, where cosmologies and mythologies were a common tool for artists as divergent as Liam Gillick, Gregor Schneider, Manfred Pernice, Andrea Zittel, Kara Walker, and of course Matthew Barney and his Yale classmates Katy Schimert, Michael Grey, and Michael Rees. Shows generated by these artists and others often used complex titling and installation strategies like books, super-graphics, and implied narratives as part of their fundamental structure. The overall effect was a collection of closed worlds, a house of doors. I was very interested in the possibilities this opened up, and after the collapse of the master narratives in the eighties, it seemed inevitable that artists

FIG. 8: MATTHEW RITCHIE INSTALLING *THE FINE CONSTANT*, 2003 AT THE CONTEMPORARY ARTS MUSEUM HOUSTON. ALL OF THE PHOTOGRAPHS ON PAGES 39–47 WERE TAKEN DURING THE INSTALLATION OF *MATTHEW RITCHIE: PROPOSITION PLAYER* AT THE CONTEMPORARY ARTS MUSEUM HOUSTON, 2003

would turn to a self-contained practice again. Typical of these projects was an implication of a larger vision, which underlay any given project. My own project was established both to take advantage of that desire and simultaneously to counter it. I created narrative structures which manifested themselves as a nonhierarchical game space, a magic square, open to multiple contradictory readings and based on an open source material from subgenres commonly relegated to the backwaters of historical curiosity, such as Gnostic angelology, unified field theory, conspiracy theories of all stripes, creation debates, and evolutionary arguments—in short, every field where the desire for a universal taxonomy, a context outside all contexts, had outweighed truth, proof, or consensus. My project was hopefully a generous construction of arguments that was always intended to be impossible to be read as any kind of closed Wagnerian master myth and to be more a kind of open, porous toolkit for thinking.

TG Unlike Matthew Barney's *Cremaster* cycle, which is often described as Wagnerian.

MR Barney was among the first artists of my generation who was not worried by his desire to include everything he wanted into his art. I had seen the work of [Robert] Rauschenberg, [Joseph] Beuys and [Sigmar] Polke and found them similarly freeing, but somehow that moment seemed lost to my generation. That was what I thought was so liberating about the early nineties: everyone seemed to say, "I'm interested in all this stuff and I'll do it all at once, from Rikrit Tiravanija's cooking to Andrea Zittel's habitats. And that was fantastic. I was never attracted to this idea that art was somehow under siege or that preserving ideas of conservative technique was some kind of resistance. Nor did the myth of infinite progression seem particularly truthful either. I think something much more interesting has happened since then. An enormous space has opened up where we can see the possibility of these radicalized, spectacularized individual projects to change and evolve, to escape from the cultic and predictable obligations of art historical expectations. Instead of accepting a relationship to the Wagnerian model, which is based on the model of traditional cult worship, I think we should be thinking about Milton, whose work was based on ideas of intellectual generosity, individual freedom, and responsibility.

FROM TOP: FIGS. 9–11

The ubiquity of cheap, low-res technology allows every artist to become their own NASA.

In other words, for me, the original idea that any sufficiently complex system would acquire its own internal meaning (information theory) has mutated into an omnivorous visualization system constantly generating multiple meanings. This system is not really being generated by me; it is a story by, for, and about everyone and everything. And so, without either failing or concluding as scheduled, my project has taken on an internal life. It has escaped. The separate characters have become highly individualized characters, places, landscapes, and organs, all competing and dreaming in an endless conceptual war consisting of endless victories for all. None of the work in the current show corresponds to the initial table of characteristics, colors, names, or functions. Instead the works all contain multiple and polluted variants and offspring of the original structure. One way to describe what I am doing is I am trying to describe and include what cannot be systematized. The classic regressions of [Bertrand] Russell's set of all sets, or the Binding Problem, or the question of a priori consciousness, or the origin of source material for the Big Bang, are all ultimately about asking what can and cannot be known. They are outside context questions.

TG What do you mean by "outside context questions"?

MR How can we perceive the structure that contains the model of our perception?

TG Do you think you have successfully given back to painting the idea of translatability? If so, isn't it only within your system?

MR I think I have sort of, but the result has turned out to be a kind of conjuring trick with only one useful function: to show that all language requires an internal consistency, not only to function but to have integrity.

TG Does critique enter into your work? Is that even a relevant question? Or desire to get out of your work?

MR Could you expand on that a little?

TG About critique? What I mean by that?

MR Yeah.

TG The belief that art is less about creativity than it is about questioning art, society, power, money, master narratives. I came out of that tradition through academia and the Whitney program in the 1980s. But the more I got to know and write about art in the '90s after I left academia, the more narrow that view became, which is why Barney's, yours, or Ellen Gallagher's work became of such interest to me. In this more generative kind of work, critique is not the impetus so much as generating new systems. Creativity returns but through the lens of a very diffracted (post-Derridean/ Haraway) space.

MR It's an interesting question because the third thing I was interested in at the beginning of this project was the idea of the *Ius Utendi*, the model of law proposed by William of Ockham (one of the first proponents of intellectual freedom), which concerns the structures and questions that underlie any self-critical, self-sustaining, open game of thought.

TG How has he appeared in your work?

MR Well Ockham is most famous for Ockham's razor, a deductive mental tool.

TG Which is?

MR The simplest solution is the likeliest one. But determining the simplest solution requires an understanding of the entire context. In Ockham's time, the simplest solution was to assume God was responsible for everything from wood floating on water to the motion of the planets. But that led to heresy because it conflicted with the idea of free will and to idiocy because the basic laws of observable science were constantly being challenged by this idea that they were "against the will of God." It's the same kind of thinking that opposes stem cell research today.

But Ockham is most interesting as an example of the power and limits of logical thinking—what you could call critique. He sin-

gle-handedly challenged the rights and limits of the papacy at a time when it was the unchallenged arbiter not only of the present, but of the spiritual future of every Christian. He won through the force of logic on what he called the "right of use," the belief that each of us has both rights and responsibilities that no larger structure can mediate for us. In short, he presents the individual as a moral ecology. Real critique must begin with an understanding of the entire system and one's personal relationship to it.

TG Okay, so now I'll come in from that other side. Your generation's reliance on baroque internal myths, or even baroque public myths (science) in your case, has been interpreted as this kind of irresponsible system, because you could be interpreted as saying, "Well, everything is meaningful and everywhere, and it can go anywhere." If that's the case, then nothing means anything, and everything's up for grabs, and it's that awful postmodernism stuff, right?

MR Well, science is hardly a myth and like any truly complex system, it demands internal integrity. But I usually get asked the opposite question instead.

TG Which is?

MR "Why do we even have to know what it means?" I've heard that thousands of times. Most people don't want to know that there's an internal architecture, or background information, and that it all holds together.

TG That's so depressing. Why can't people understand that this is what makes the art so interesting. Certainly it's what is strong and breathtaking about yours and Barney's.

MR The criticism of complexity is based on this unfortunate idea that we in the visual arts should be afraid to make big, beautiful, complex things in case we somehow "alienate" a frightened and timid potential audience. I do not underestimate the audience in that way. It's so odd. The same people that worry about contemporary art in this way are completely unafraid of the Sistine Chapel, or *The Matrix*, or jet planes, which are much more complicated. Part of the premise of this show was the idea of shared and lost infor-

FROM TOP: FIGS. 12–14

mation, so to make the heads for *The Fine Constant*, I worked with ten-year-olds in Houston and New York, and they were not alienated by the complexity; they embraced it. They were less confused than anyone I worked with. So I think any audience can and will rise to the challenge of complex work as long as they feel they can trust the artist's integrity. This is the most important thing, because only an internal integrity can guarantee an implicit order that transcends these kinds of questions.

TG That's excellent.

MR There are also big differences between the various types of work that suffer from the criticism of complexity or hermeticism. You are the Barney scholar here, but it seems to me his work is based on the idea of constructing a mythology. It builds upon itself. He's forcing a kind of concentration on the viewer. Someone like Beuys was interested in placing himself at the center of a postwar absence, and his meaning system was a conduit with himself as the social lubricant. Kara Walker, on the other hand, seems to be more interested in an epic David Lean-like portrayal that focuses less on one individual than on articulating the giant voice of moral betrayal. Whereas what I'm interested in is an opening up of consciousness, a reversion, a reversal, so that what happens to viewers is they think about things from the outside through the context. Information becomes the material, the form. So I see the paintings and all the things that I'm making as parts of something like a telescope. I'm trying to create a class of objects whose main property is that they turn the viewer's consciousness back out. All the information in my work can be found in the public realm, on the Internet or at any public library, but what *I try* to deliver is the idea of personal intellectual freedom, the right to think any thought on any scale.

TG In previous interviews you talk about how important it is that the systems you are exploring are real, i.e., part of the public or social order. The abstract, self-made, total fantasy system of the *Cremaster* is your exact opposite. You start with the rules in the universe that determine us as a game and watch the story grow.

FROM TOP: FIGS. 15–17

MR Yes, we are all an expression of the game. We are part of a particular spread of cards, and those cards are going to be reshuffled

tomorrow and the day after. This is the hand you've been dealt, so it's up to you to make a story out of the random insane collection of things that are happening to you right now.

TG It seems like your story of life has an awful lot to do with rules, doesn't it? Would you say, for you, rules are almost the primary material?

MR Wow, that's a really rich question. Especially since a good part of my life was about circumventing rules. [Laughing] And I'd really like *them* to answer it for you. [Ritchie hands her "The Rules of the Game" (p. 57).]

TG Are you kidding?

MR No. You are right—the relationship between the rules and the information, between signal and noise, is the question. It's the question for everything. Not just for art making, but life. Life is about rules. You can say you "don't want to learn," but you have to learn about gravity. You have to learn about food and water, and then you have to learn about social life to keep getting food and water. The rules that we tend to think are the most important end up being, in the larger picture, nothing compared to the fundamental rules of your own life. Like when you will die. The whole point about rules is that they are what allow you to play the game. But just because you know the rules doesn't mean the game is any more predictable, or any less fun, or any less absorbing. You know you're going to win and lose, and that's what counts.

TG Most rules aren't about learning, just obeying. One doesn't have to understand or even know about gravity, but one does have to obey it.

MR Yeah, that is certainly what we have been told. But who told you that, and why? The new show is very much about this. Like, in the end, is a story really more about its rules? Is it all about the setup? Or can we look at all the rules at once?

TG Of any one moment in time, a person—anything? Why is that important? What does one get by seeing all the rules at once?

MR Everything. All those rules are conspiring in a nonhierarchical space, where everything is potentially observable at the same time. Maybe the rules are just another way of asking what will happen next?

TG Which is the fundamental structure or definition of narrative. But what you are talking about is more about breaking through all the dimensions and seeing everything at once. Maybe it's the word "rules" that throws me. Is there another word for what you're talking about?

MR Yes, there are lots because I don't even think what I'm interested in is about "rules" in the narrow sense. I'm really looking at the fundamental properties in nature (that are sometimes called constants) that underlie everything. Laws tend to express the relationships of constants. But the other thing that's specifically interesting to me, in terms of what you're asking about, is that every individual person is building his or her own information mass, and although each mass is derived from the laws underlying most of the universe, everybody becomes their own set of dice—or their own pack of cards. We are all making our own rules—in defiance of the underlying ones.

TG The difference between the pre-information age and post is precisely this issue of open access to "all" knowledge. We suffer from what William Gibson calls "information sickness." Survival of the fittest is no longer who is the one who knows everything, because everybody can do that to some extent via the Internet and technology. But power or success or achievement or breakthrough comes from the ingenuity in how one makes sense of the information. In your model, it is what roll of the dice or division of cards each person develops.

MR Yes, when you have a new experience, the hippocampus actually rebuilds itself. Information, new information, literally makes the brain change shape. They've been doing these studies recently with monks that show the alpha brain waves calm down during meditation. The hippocampus actually changes shape. Buddhist monks and people who don't meditate have brains that actually work differently. It's actually a physical change. So every day we're making a map of our life in our brain. We're doing what we're talking about in a very abstract way, processing everything into a physical object, inside our heads, every day.

TG So one can look at your work as as much a kind of map of the brain, and not just the idea of the universe and the cosmos? You put it beautifully in 1997 in the Jennifer Berman interview: "… you've got hundreds of competing impulses—your skin is itching, you're responding to pressures and thoughts of your age, your body is deteriorating, you're going to the gym. It's a mess. This temple of activity. This hive. The heart's beating, you can hear it ticking in the back of your mind. And your brain, god knows what's going on in there. No one's even close to figuring that out. And so this is an attempt to try and map what it is like to be a person."

MR Yeah.

TG Have you ever experienced the sense of your brain growing?

MR Oh, God, yeah! And not just taking drugs. If you pay attention, you can feel it all the time.

TG But isn't that amazing? I remember the point when I felt my brain matter growing. There was this feeling, literally, of more stuff going in and growing, and I could understand things I couldn't before.

MR Yeah. That's amazing. And then the real trick is you've got to figure out a shape for it all. Like will the form the information takes become a useful tool—like a personal cosmology—or more important, can you make it into something you can use or at least tolerate?

TG Tolerate is an interesting word. It's about finding a level we can tolerate in the sense of a threshold we make, manage, and use. Otherwise information saturation becomes painful, and as Gibson says, we get sick! Is that what your paintings do? Are they ways of tolerating information overload?

MR I think so. Raw information has the ability to cause real disorientation. Information has to be cooked. The paintings are a kind of immune system; literally pictures of thinking.

FROM TOP: FIGS. 18–19

TG Like what hydrogen actually looks like if it turns into knowledge?

MR Yes.

TG And yet, color and line are your vocabulary. Color's the most important element, in a way, right? Are there specific associations with each color?

MR Well, originally there were seven colors with very specific hues that were in fact directly related to certain ideas I had about color theory. But then as they started to bleed and cross-mingle and procreate with each other, it was like all these children emerged. Children in the form of really dirty colors. But in truth, I would say that formally the paintings rely as much on the idea of "fill" as they do on color.

TG Territories.

MR Yes, in a way this goes back to the map and to the problem of how to contain or shape information. There's actually a mechanical model of how much information one can contain in a space, based on the number of colors and how dense they are. It's why maps look the way they do. They're not brightly colored all over because, if so, you wouldn't be able to look at and read them anymore. So when I was figuring out how to make these paintings, I had all these books on color. There was this book called *Envisioning Information*,[2] which is very famous. It is all about how to make good and bad models for presenting information.

TG And yours, are they good or bad models?

MR I think mine are terrible models. [Laughter]

TG Now why is that? Why would that be more compelling for you than doing "good" models?

MR Well, a "good" model for information is one where it's totally legible to any person, for instance, a train schedule. Such models shouldn't be confusing but completely ordered.

FROM TOP: FIGS. 20–21

TG So, good models for presenting information are by definition not very interesting art. If so, where does your work stand? Or why work within these boundaries, which seem to contradict one another? What I'm getting at is, you seem caught between representing or modeling information via painting and making art. Art and information seem to be totally at odds, and yet those are the two things you are working with!

MR Well, a train schedule is very limited—its presentation of order relies on the absence of all other information. The real world is also a terrible model for presenting important information since it includes everything. But this project, as it stands in the Houston show, represents a kind of crisis, climax, or collapse of the earlier way of working precisely because of this conflict. For me this is an attempt to take advantage of the energy released as the first wave generated in 1995 comes crashing down. From this conflict, an alternate ecology, an ecology of information, has emerged, casting spaces against time, matter, energy. This ecology, rather than the initial rules, has emerged from inside the whole project. Rather than an episodic recapitulation of previous stories and structures, this show seeks to collapse all the categories, characters, and stories into one moment—a moment where the viewer can enter and begin to play the game him or herself. This entire show was also built around the idea of participation from the very beginning, not only from the side of the viewer, but also from the side of the maker. I wanted to explore how information as a material could be scaled and worked with by different kinds of collaborators using different technologies. I wanted to see how much could be lost and then regained as I scaled the different elements. So I worked with a totally diverse team of collaborators around the country who were each making a component, like the programmer making the game in California, or mold makers casting dice from prehistoric elk bones at the American Museum of Natural History, or ten-year-old children making the heads in Houston from Sculpy, or the water-jet cutter putting the sculpture together in his barn. I wanted part of the process to be about breaking this system of mine into parts and surrendering it to chance in the hands of others. This way the idea of a scalable language could really be tested out in practice. And their independent decisions ended up directly influencing the paintings and drawings, returning me to this idea of an endlessly

2. Edward Tufte, *Envisioning Information* (Cheshire, Connecticut: Graphics Press, 1990).

opening, collapsing and infinitely generous structure. In terms of the viewers' experience too, I have made it participatory. For instance, there is an interactive digital craps game, and there's this pack of cards that I'm making. It's a pack of all the characters, the forty-nine characters. So everyone who comes can play the game. [Ritchie pulls out a pack of cards.]

TG You have the pack of fifty-two Most Wanted Iraqi cards. Wait, this is your color—these are your colors?!

MR No, these are the U.S. government colors.

TG Give me a break!

MR Funny, that is. [Laughs.]

TG So, you did dodge the question about the meaning of your color scheme, because there is a kind of army green throughout your world of color.

MR No, it's just coincidence.

TG It's just a coincidence?

MR People use these colors because they're heavy on white. They're cheap.

TG Okay, so talk about your craps game and cards. How do they function in the show?

MR You come into the show and are given a playing card with a character on it. But the show is not about all the characters. It's not like they're all over the walls or anything. There are also four suits in a pack of cards. So, now you've got forty-nine characters, and they're divided into seven families each, and then they're divided into four suits, which splits them up into their functionality. And the four suits represent the four basic forces of the universe. (Which, by the way, were never included in the original seven families or the basic characters or properties, because I didn't know enough to include them. Thank goodness.) So now, literally, these characters

build the stories, but the stories are only a superstructure placed on top of the underlying structure, which is these four basic forces of the universe, and they then build through the craps game into a central figure, "the swimmer," that ties everything together.

TG You mean these forces are undeniable?

MR We describe the universe through four forces that make up everything. The Weak Force, which is radiation, the Strong Force, which holds atoms together, Gravity, which holds the universe together, and Electromagnetism—most commonly understood as light.

TG Is that four because there are only four? Or have you chosen just four?

MR No, I hardly ever need to make anything up. There really are four forces that combine to make everything, including the four constants represented here: $e=$ the elementary charge, $c=$ the speed of light, $G=$ the constant of gravity, and $h=$ the constant of action. For this book we made those letters each one of the four colors.

TG So according to Big Science, there are four?

MR You're having a hard time with this aren't you. Well, the theory is that they were all once one force—before the Big Bang, but there are lots more fours, just as there were lots of sevens when I needed them. You know, four seasons, four directions of the compass, four suits of cards. They're all actually dependent on each other. The four forces also generate the four fixed units of measurement. So they're all completely contingent on each other.

TG So, how does all of this work in your show?

MR The viewer walks in, gets one of these cards and then gives it to a guy at the gaming table. He then gives them the digital dice, which are four-sided dice cast from prehistoric animal bones, and then they play the digital craps game. And as they play the game they build the paintings.

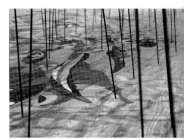

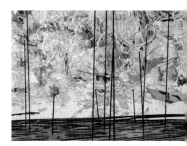

FROM TOP: FIGS. 22–24

TG Literally? During the show? How does that happen? Where's "the painter," meaning you? And why are the dice prehistoric animal bones?

MR The first dice ever used were astragals—ankle bones of a cloven hoofed animal. They are four-sided and were what were first used as dice, so in this case they're cast from prehistoric giant elk ankle bones. They have four sides. One dice has four numbers and one has the four symbols of the suits: spades, clubs, hearts, diamonds—and they're colored. Blue is spades, green is clubs, and so on.

I also made a one-person craps table that serves as a projection surface. You throw the dice onto the table and they have tiny computers inside them that register what you throw and send a radio signal to a computer above. The computer then builds and projects random animated elements from a digital game onto the surface of the table, depending on your score. The evolution of the game resembles the main sequence of the paintings. Another version of the game, based on the same dice throw but using the random quality of the game to build a different image, is being projected on the wall as you play.

The game has five levels, because it's also based on the voodoo universe, which has five levels and because voodoo is the only chance-based religion that I could come across.

TG This is all sounding like mad associative ranting.

MR And yet this is how I think. In voodoo you pray to a certain kind of god, but you might get another god coming in and at you. It's also the only one where the universe invests itself in you, rather than you having to pray to it; it is an inverted religion. And it's sort of related to Christianity, which is something that I think is a legitimate context for me to be allowed to associate with. So anyway, to return to the show, if you do all these strange things in the gaming room, alternate versions of the structures of the paintings will build themselves in front of you each time.

TG How does one win?

MR Winning has to do with acquiring enough light and gravity and mass to get to the next level. It's really just about play.

FROM TOP: FIGS. 25–26

TG What if the first person who comes in ends up playing the whole time the show's up?

MR Well, that's great! But there is an end to it. *Proposition Player* goes through five stages, evolving from the first diagram, which is the underlying structure of the universe, to a painting, which is the evolution of atoms, and then, at the end, a figure emerges out of all of them, built out of the same parts.

TG Is there another metaphor besides "game" that works for you?

MR I think "life" is a good metaphor. [Laughs] Or going back to the word I used before: "context." Because all rules are interdependent on each other, they build a context. Light is dependent on nuclear fusion, which is dependent on the space/time structure of the universe, which is dependent on gravity. In other words, everything is linked together in a chain, in a context, which is the game. The game is much more than just the rules of the game. It's the whole thing. If you take out one part, one rule, the whole game collapses. So if that happens, how do you represent the context?

TG Like an organism. Is context another name for history?

MR The real context is the structure that contains the model of our perception that we think is the context—it is the framework that allows the rules of the game to be rules. So, how do you step outside a context that includes everything? This is the thing that I'm always talking about. It is this defining problem: context as theory. How do you represent the presence of the defining absence?

TG Defining absence, there's a great definition of God. In a way, for you to talk about history is off the mark because history, as a system for making sense of the events of experience, is really just another kind of perception?

MR We can only see 5% of the universe. We've called another 25% "dark energy" and the remaining 70% "dark matter." We're working from a model with 95% of the information missing—so no wonder everybody's acting like they're in the dark. So the big question for me is: how do you visually represent that absence?

In *The Fine Constant*, each of the heads is based on a sculpture made by a ten-year-old in Houston who participated in a workshop based on my stories. The heads were decimated by a computer: we scanned the original head, turned it into polygons and reduced the polygons by 95%. This whole fabrication process was intended to represent the radical and persistent information loss that characterizes human experience and to show how in a way, it doesn't matter.

TG Yikes!

MR And despite the fact that these heads derive from a story told to a child, who made a sculpture of the story that was then reduced by 95% in detail and then cast—we still have enough to understand it as a head! So the universe is still legible. It's still working for you, even when you can only see 5% of what is there. But truthfully, as human beings, we can probably only even grasp about 5% of that visible universe. So we discard another 95% and make our daily decisions based on 5% of the available information we have left and yet we still feel the rightness of it all. Even though we're only able to see only one quarter of one percent, we still feel we are connected to the underlying order. We can go further and further down in resolution, but as long as the underlying grain remains true, we can be convinced we are connected to the whole—we can ignore the overwhelming absence.

TG Sounds like the Bush administration.

MR But it's how all of our information is produced. It's like, how can you think about your own consciousness from outside your brain? I was making yet more Sculpy heads at a charity event and another ten-year-old came up to me during the workshop and said, "I want to make a model of the universe." And I thought, "Did someone send you to me? Is this a setup? You know, Candid Camera?" And then she said, "No, okay, the universe is too big. Let's make the solar system." And I was like, "Okay—phew!" And then she said, "But what does the universe look like anyway?" And all I could say was, "Good question." I mean, isn't that it? There she was, age ten, standing outside the universe going, "And so, what does this look like? How can I put it altogether all at once?"

TG And to her it wasn't a game

MR No, to her it was just like, life.

FIG. 27

100%   5%   5% of 5%

We can only see 5% of the universe. We've called another 25% "dark energy" and the remaining 70% "dark matter." We're working from a model with 95% of the information missing—so no wonder everybody's acting like they're in the dark. So the big question for me is: how do you visually represent that absence?

In *The Fine Constant*, each of the heads is based on a sculpture made by a ten-year-old in Houston who participated in a workshop based on my stories. The heads were decimated by a computer: we scanned the original head, turned it into polygons and reduced the polygons by 95%. This whole fabrication process was intended to represent the radical and persistent information loss that characterizes human experience and to show how in a way, it doesn't matter. —Matthew Ritchie

ABOVE: PHOTOGRAPH OF JEREMY KING AND ONE OF THE HEADS HE CREATED IN COLLABORATION WITH MATTHEW RITCHIE AT, LEFT TO RIGHT, 100% OF ORIGINAL INFORMATION IN THE PHOTOGRAPH, 5% OR THE ORIGINAL INFORMATION, AND 5% OF 5% OF THE ORIGINAL INFORMATION

RIGHT: *THE FINE CONSTANT* (DETAIL), 2003. JEREMY KING'S SCULPTED HEAD REDUCED TO 5% OF THE ORIGINAL INFORMATION

FOLLOWING PAGES (PP. 50–51): *THE FINE CONSTANT* (DETAILS), 2003. POWDERCOATED ALUMINUM. STEEL, GYPSUM, WAX, ENAMEL. 95 x 1,152 x 192 INCHES (241 x 2926 x 488 CM). COURTESY THE ARTIST AND ANDREA ROSEN GALLERY, NEW YORK

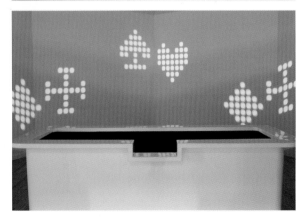
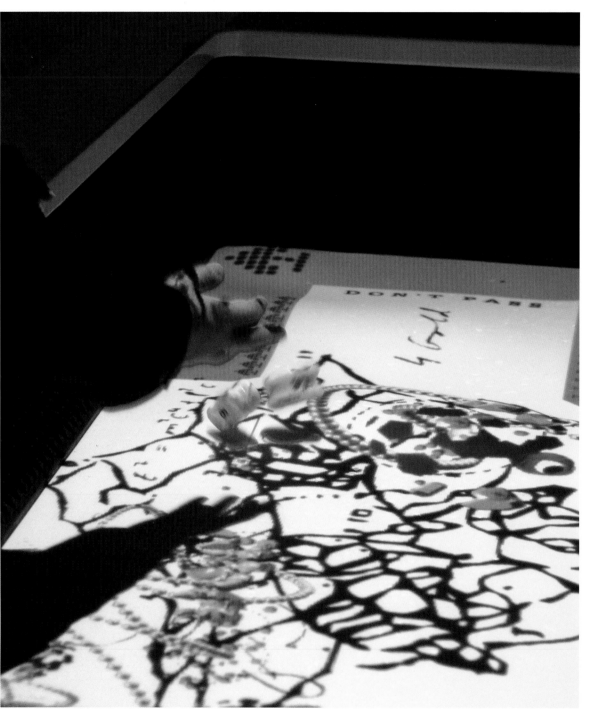

PREVIOUS PAGES, THIS PAGE: *PROPOSITION PLAYER* (DETAILS), 2003. POWDERCOATED ALUMINUM, MINICEL FOAM, RUBBER, ADHESIVE, ELECTRONIC COMPONENTS, ONE PAIR CAST RESIN DICE, AND CUSTOM-DESIGNED DECK OF PLAYING CARDS.
42 x 42 x 98 INCHES (107 x 107 x 249 CM). COURTESY THE ARTIST AND ANDREA ROSEN GALLERY

RULES:

There are four suits in the deck:

- Diamonds: representing money
- Hearts: representing love
- Clubs: representing growth
- Spades: representing conflict

LEVEL 1: THE FUNCTION SUITE

There are four forces underlying the physical structure of the universe:

- Strong Force
- Weak Force
- Gravitational Force
- Electromagnetic Force

LEVEL 2: THE BOX FACTORY

There are four basic units of measurement:

- Mass
- Linear Time
- Length
- Temperature

LEVEL 3: THE ANTI CITY

There are four main players in atomic reactions:

- Quarks & Electrons (Fermions)
- W/Z Particles
- Gluons
- Photons

LEVEL 4: THE NEW PLACE

There are four thermodynamic states:

- Enthalpy
- Entropy
- Energy
- Equilibrium

LEVEL 5: THE SLOW TIDE

There are four nucleic acids in DNA:

- Thymine
- Adenine
- Cytosine
- Guanine

YOUR PROGRESS THROUGH THE GAME IS DETERMINED BY CHANCE.

Four points of each suit must be rolled to reach the next level.

Both die must be rolled each time.

- 6 is a natural
- 4 is a pass
- 3 is a don't pass
- 1 is craps

YOU MAY ALREADY BE A WINNER.

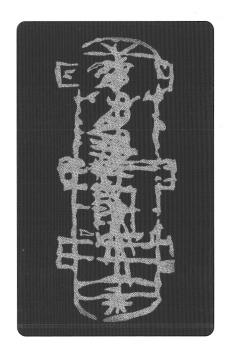

THE STRONG FORCE / GLUONS

A

h / THE CONSTANT OF ACTION = 6.6 x 10^-34 J.s

THE GAMBLERS / THE FUNCTION ROOM

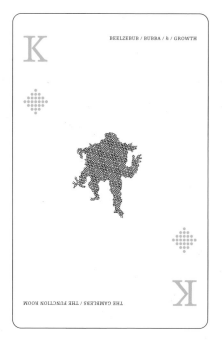

BEELZEBUB / BUBBA / h / GROWTH

K

THE GAMBLERS / THE FUNCTION ROOM

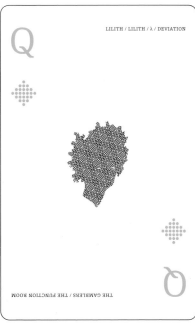

LILITH / LILITH / λ / DEVIATION

Q

THE GAMBLERS / THE FUNCTION ROOM

EN SOPH / BABY / H / EQUILIBRIUM

J

THE FAST SET / THE NEW PLACE

PENUMUE / PENNY / TEMPORAL / LEARNING

10

THE WATCHERS / THE HARD WAY

ABOVE AND PAGES 58–63: *PROPOSITION PLAYER* (DETAIL: DECK OF CARDS), 2003. INK ON CARD. 3 1/2 x 2 1/2 INCHES (9 X 6.5 CM) EACH. COURTESY THE ARTIST AND ANDREA ROSEN GALLERY, NEW YORK

9 — SHEMJAZA / MJ / LIMBIC / REPENTANCE

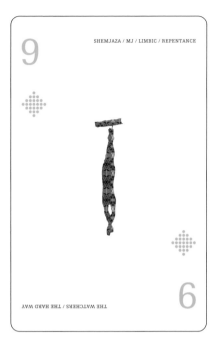

THE WATCHERS / THE HARD WAY

8 — OCH / O.C.H. / PLANTAE / LAW

THE ROYAL FAMILY / THE FAMILY FARM

7 — RAHAB / ROBBERY / REPLICATION / VIOLENCE

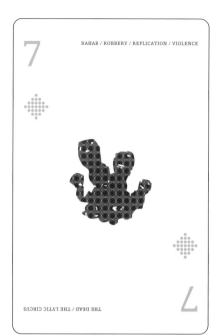

THE DEAD / THE LYTIC CIRCUS

6 — SCHIEKRON / RAPE / INFECTION / FALSE LOVE

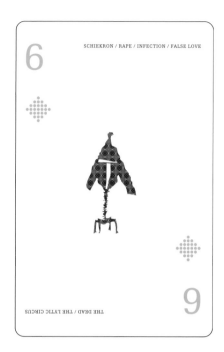

THE DEAD / THE LYTIC CIRCUS

5 — RAPHAEL / OFFICER V. RAFFI / Au / MERCY

THE DAY WATCH / THE ANTI CITY

4 — GABRIEL / CSI G. DI ANGELIS / Ag / REVELATION

THE DAY WATCH / THE ANTI CITY

3 — TAMUEL / TAMARA / ι / CHANCE

THE WORKING GROUP / THE BOX FACTORY

2 — MIHR / MIRA / M / LOYALTY

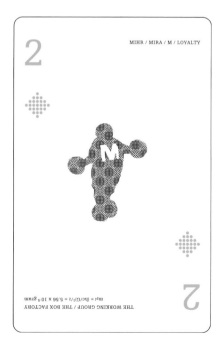

THE WORKING GROUP / THE BOX FACTORY

$m_{pl} = (\hbar c/G)^{1/2} = 5.56 \times 10^{-5}$ gram

A (Hearts)

THE WEAK FORCE / W & Z BOSONS

e / THE ELEMENTARY CHARGE = 1.6 × 10⁻¹⁹C

K (Hearts)

K

SATAN-EL / STANLEY / Ψ / DUALITY

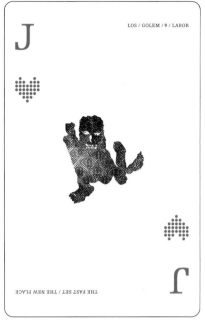

THE GAMBLERS / THE FUNCTION ROOM

Q (Hearts)

Q

LEVIATHAN / SNAKES / S / CHAOS

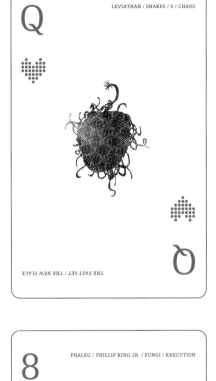

THE FAST SET / THE NEW PLACE

J (Hearts)

J

LOS / GOLEM / φ / LABOR

THE FAST SET / THE NEW PLACE

10 (Hearts)

10

KOKOBEL / COCA / PARIETAL / DISTANCE

THE WATCHERS / THE HARD WAY

9 (Hearts)

9

AZAZEL / AZZER / MEDULLA / ERROR

THE WATCHERS / THE HARD WAY

8 (Hearts)

8

PHALEG / PHILLIP KING JR. / FUNGI / EXECUTION

THE ROYAL FAMILY / THE FAMILY FARM

7 (Hearts)

7

ARATRON / ARTHUR KING / ARCHAEA / CREATION

THE ROYAL FAMILY / THE FAMILY FARM

6
NERGAL / TERRORISM / SUBSTITUTION / FEVER

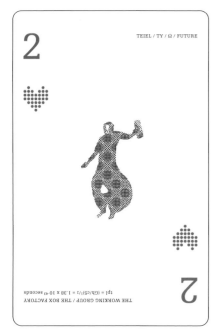

THE DEAD / THE LYTIC CIRCUS

5
MICHAEL / DET. M. DI ANGELIS / Hg / REDEMPTION

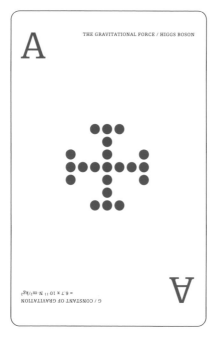

THE DAY WATCH / THE ANTI CITY

4
SAMMAEL / OFFICER S. MORDEN / Fe / DEATH

THE DAY WATCH / THE ANTI CITY

3
DOKIEL / DUKE / R / JUDGEMENT

THE WORKING GROUP / THE BOX FACTORY

2
TEIEL / TY / Ω / FUTURE

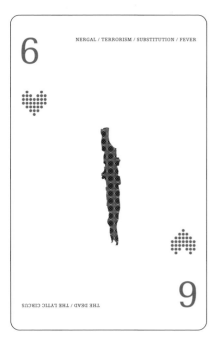

THE WORKING GROUP / THE BOX FACTORY

$t_{pl} = (Gh/c5)^{1/2} = 1.38 \times 10^{-43}$ seconds

A
THE GRAVITATIONAL FORCE / HIGGS BOSON

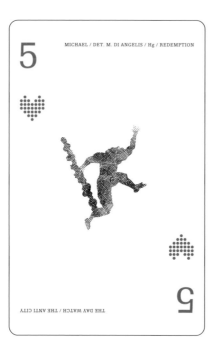

G / CONSTANT OF GRAVITATION
$= 6.7 \times 10^{-11}$ N·m²/kg²

K
ABADDON / ABADDON / O / APOCALYPSE

THE GAMBLERS / THE FUNCTION ROOM

Q
MIXIS / ACTRESS / E / FEMALE FORCE

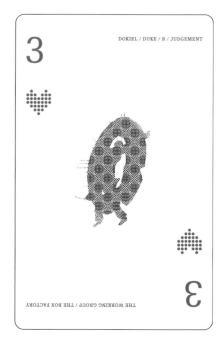

THE FAST SET / THE NEW PLACE

J
DYNAMIS / ASTRONAUT / G / MALE FORCE

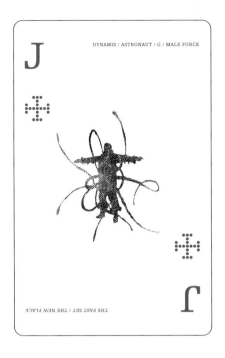

THE FAST SET / THE NEW PLACE
J

10
MULCIBER / MULLIGAN / FRONTAL / ASSEMBLY

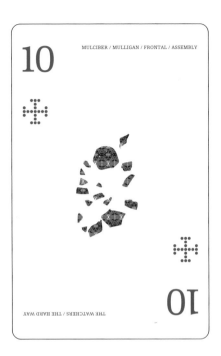

THE WATCHERS / THE HARD WAY
10

9
BETHOR / BETH KING / ANIMALIA / LEGISLATION

THE ROYAL FAMILY / THE FAMILY FARM
9

8
OPHIEL / SOPHIE KING / MONERA / CULTURE

THE ROYAL FAMILY / THE FAMILY FARM
8

7
PHUL / DR. PHILLIP KING / VIRI / TRIBE

THE ROYAL FAMILY / THE FAMILY FARM
7

6
BELPHEGOR / FRAUD / ADSORPTION / DISCOVERY

THE DEAD / THE LYTIC CIRCUS
6

5
CASSIEL / CMDR. CASSIUS KING / Pb / SOLITUDE

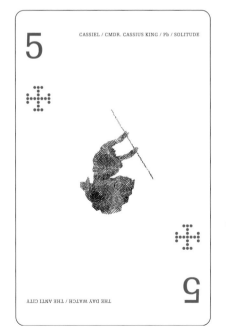

THE DAY WATCH / THE ANTI CITY
5

4
ANAEL / DET. A. ELIZARDO / Cu / SEXUALITY

THE DAY WATCH / THE ANTI CITY
4

3 — ASTORETH / ASTA / x / AMBIGUITY
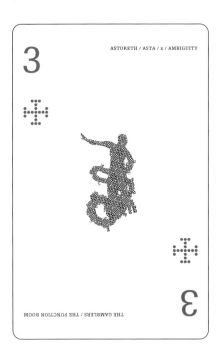
THE GAMBLERS / THE FUNCTION ROOM

2 — SOURIEL / SOUR / V / ANNUNCIATION
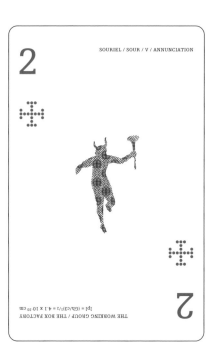
THE WORKING GROUP / THE BOX FACTORY
$lpl = (Gh/c3)1/2 = 4.1 \times 10^{-33}$ cm

A — THE ELECTROMAGNETIC FORCE / PHOTON

c / THE SPEED OF LIGHT = 3.0×10^8 m/s

K — LUCIFER / LUCKY / γ / FREE WILL
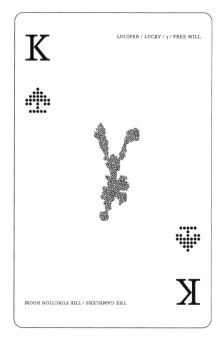
THE GAMBLERS / THE FUNCTION ROOM

Q — PISTIS SOPHIA / MLLE FLORIDA / K / WISDOM
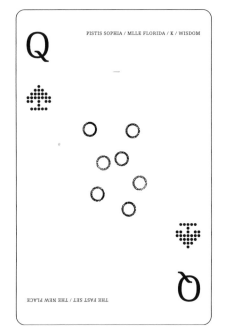
THE FAST SET / THE NEW PLACE

J — ABRAXAS / SWIMMER / ∞ / INFINITY
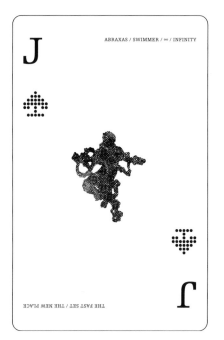
THE FAST SET / THE NEW PLACE

10 — TAMAII / TAM / OCCIPITAL / CONTRAST

THE WATCHERS / THE HARD WAY

9 — KASHDEJAH / CASH / CEREBELLUM / CONTROL
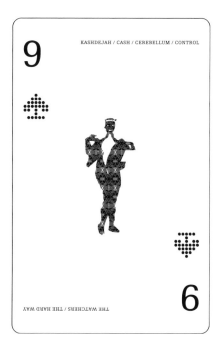
THE WATCHERS / THE HARD WAY

8 — HAGITH / THE HAG / PROTISTA / SOCIETY
THE ROYAL FAMILY / THE FAMILY FARM

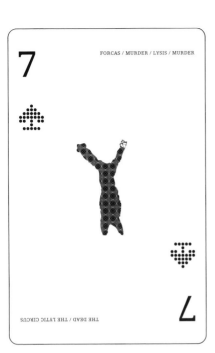

7 — FORCAS / MURDER / LYSIS / MURDER
THE DEAD / THE LYTIC CIRCUS

6 — MASTEMA / RIOT / TRANSCRIPTION / ANIMOSITY
THE DEAD / THE LYTIC CIRCUS

5 — BELIAR / TREASON / DISEASE / DECEPTION
THE DEAD / THE LYTIC CIRCUS

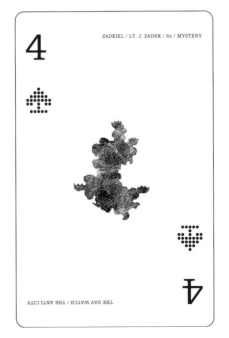

4 — ZADKIEL / LT. J. ZADEK / Sn / MYSTERY
THE DAY WATCH / THE ANTI CITY

3 — OMAEL / MA / Σ/ι / REPRODUCTION
THE WORKING GROUP / THE BOX FACTORY

2 — METATRON / META / T / MEMORY
THE WORKING GROUP / THE BOX FACTORY
$T_{pl} = k^{-1}(hc^5/G)^{1/2} = 3.5 \times 10^{-32}$ Kelvin

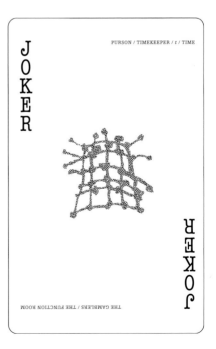

JOKER — PURSON / TIMEKEEPER / t / TIME
THE GAMBLERS / THE FUNCTION ROOM

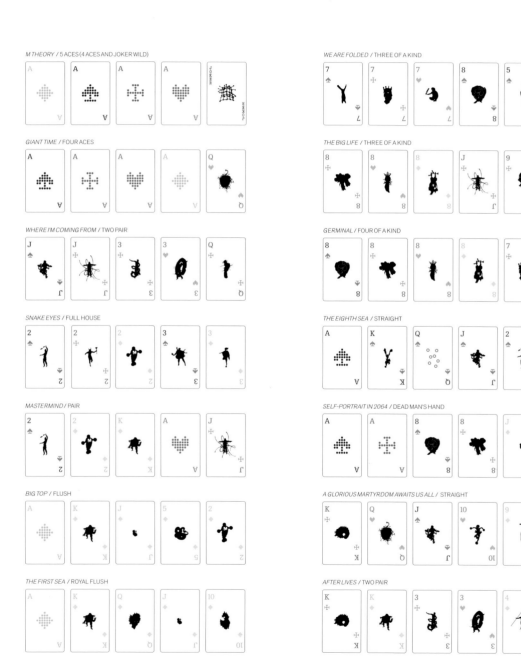

The following paintings together form what Matthew Ritchie calls "The Main Sequence," a series of works that began in 1998 with *Lucky* (fig. 32) and concludes with *Afterlives* (2002). The series follows the same object, the universe, as it transforms over time. Though the episodes of this "story" were not painted in sequential order, they are presented here in order. All works are included in the exhibition unless otherwise indicated.

Using the deck of cards created for *Proposition Player*, Ritchie has linked a poker hand to each painting. In addition to the traditional numbers and suits in each hand, characters and attributes assigned to each card by Ritchie also play a role in the painting.

M THEORY, 2000. OIL AND MARKER ON CANVAS. 81 3/4 x 109 3/4 INCHES (208 x 275 CM). L A C – SWITZERLAND (NOT IN EXHIBITION)

GIANT TIME, 2003. OIL AND MARKER ON CANVAS. 99 x 132 INCHES (251 x 335 CM). PRIVATE COLLECTION, NEW YORK

WHERE I'M COMING FROM, 2003. OIL AND MARKER ON CANVAS. 99 x 121 INCHES (251 x 307 CM). COLLECTION JOHN A. SMITH AND VICKY HUGHES

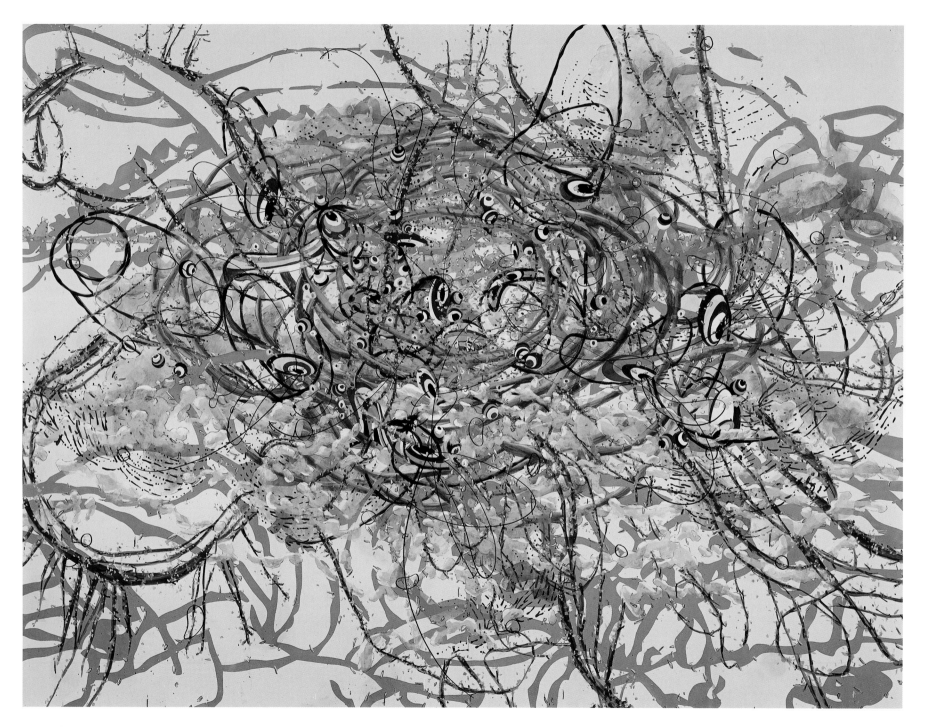

SNAKE EYES, 2003. OIL AND MARKER ON CANVAS. 99 x 132 INCHES (251 x 335 CM). COURTESY THE ARTIST AND ANDREA ROSEN GALLERY, NEW YORK

MASTERMIND, 2002. OIL AND MARKER ON CANVAS. 88 x 121 INCHES (223 x 307 CM). PRIVATE COLLECTION, BOLOGNA, ITALY (NOT IN EXHIBITION)

BIG TOP, 2000. OIL AND MARKER ON CANVAS. 84 x 96 INCHES (213 x 244 CM). MARC AND LIVIA STRAUSS FAMILY COLLECTION (NOT IN EXHIBITION)

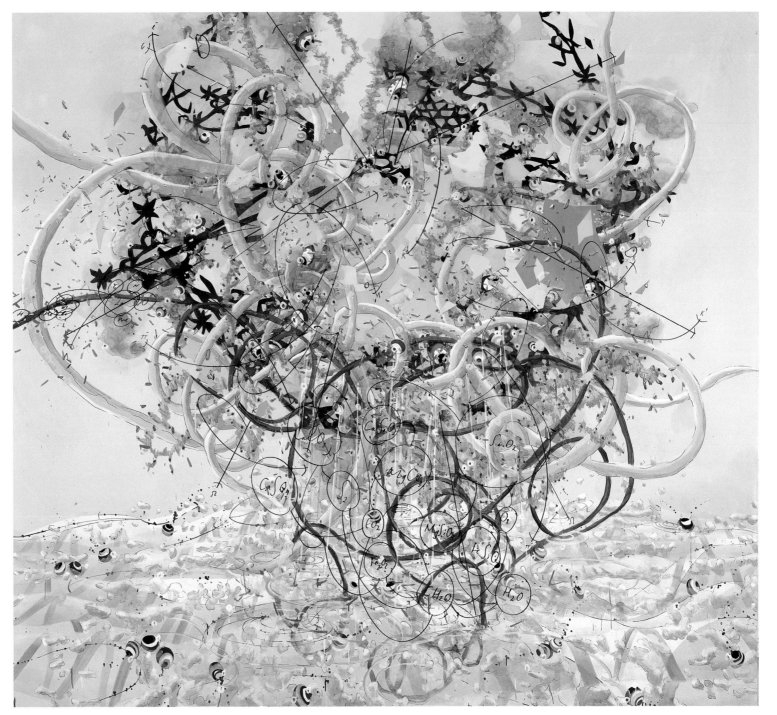

THE FIRST SEA, 2003. OIL AND MARKER ON CANVAS. 99 x 110 INCHES (251 x 279 CM). PHIL SCHRAGER COLLECTION, OMAHA

WE ARE FOLDED, 2002. OIL AND MARKER ON CANVAS. 88 x 121 INCHES (224 x 307 CM). DIMITRIS DASKALOPOULOS COLLECTION, GREECE

THE BIG LIFE, 2002. OIL AND MARKER ON CANVAS. 88 x 154 INCHES (223 x 391 CM). COLLECTION JOHN KALDOR, SYDNEY, AUSTRALIA

GERMINAL, 2001. OIL AND MARKER ON CANVAS. 72 x 120 INCHES (183 x 305 CM). THYSSEN-BORNEMISZA ART CONTEMPORARY, VIENNA (NOT IN EXHIBITION)

THE EIGHTH SEA, 2002. OIL AND MARKER ON CANVAS, 99 x 121 INCHES (251 x 307 CM). COLLECTION THE ARTIST

SELF-PORTRAIT IN 2064, 2003. OIL AND MARKER ON CANVAS. 80 x 100 INCHES (203 x 254 CM). COLLECTION NINAH AND MICHAEL LYNNE

A GLORIOUS MARTYRDOM AWAITS US ALL AT THE HANDS OF OUR TENDER AND MERCIFUL GOD, 2003. OIL AND MARKER ON CANVAS, 88 x 99 INCHES (224 x 251 CM). COURTESY THE ARTIST, ANDREA ROSEN GALLERY, NEW YORK, AND C/O ATLE GERHARDSEN, BERLIN

ABOVE: *AFTER LIVES*, 2002. OIL AND MARKER ON CANVAS. 88 x 154 INCHES (224 x 391 CM). COLLECTION ALLISON AND NEIL RUBLER

OPPOSITE: *AFTER LIVES* (DETAIL), 2002

Laura Steward Heon

Riffs in Pidgin:
The Thermodynamic Aesthetics of Matthew Ritchie

That Matthew Ritchie's cosmological portfolio appears to be tidy, systematic, even linguistic in its arrangement and orderliness has attracted the notice of curious viewers since his first exhibition *Working Model*, in 1995. In the eight years between that exhibition and that of the dazzlingly complex *Proposition Player*, entropy has chipped away at order, even as the linguistic quality of his work has been conserved. The paintings, drawings, games, sculptures, books, and wall drawings have limbered up over time, embracing the poetic potential of entropy and chance more closely. Understanding this transformation in Ritchie's work requires us to separate the cosmology or continuum or project or what-you-will that he codified initially in *Working Model* from the individual pieces that have made it up over the years.

Ritchie has often discussed his desire to make painting a complete working system that others could clearly understand, that is, to bring it into the realm of language. Given this project's linguistic character, perhaps linguistics can offer useful tools to effect the separation between system and speech; to wit, *langue* and *parole*. In Saussurean linguistics, *langue*, best described as "language system," means the totality of regularities and pattern that underlie language behavior; *parole*, or "language behavior," is the actual utterances themselves. Here, *langue* would refer to Ritchie's total project (his cosmological portfolio), and *parole* to the separate works.

The linguistic quality is most readily apparent in a work included in the *Working Model* exhibition, an eponymous chart, which was exhibited with a small wooden sculpture called *The God Game* (1995, p. 116). *Working Model* (1995, p. 116) listed the contents of Ritchie's cosmological portfolio, establishing the set of symbols and relationships that acted as vocabulary and syntax for much of

Ritchie's work of the late '90s. It was proposed as a map, a schematic drawn largely from material that, though sometimes eccentric and obscure, is also freely available to a general audience with access to any public library or the Internet. By studying this chart, should his viewers want to, they could theoretically learn what he knows in order to "read" the works. This innate accessibility is of critical importance: there is no such thing as a language with just one speaker. For Saussure, *langue* is a socially constructed system of language shaped by the totality of its speaking participants. In Ritchie's case, this shared social context comes about in two ways: first, through the open source material that serves as the basis for the *langue*, and secondly, through the interactive games, like *The God Game* in *Working Model* or the digital dice game (pp. 52–54) at the heart of *Proposition Player*, that each site-specific version of the project incorporates. These games are the forums where the language is spoken, where viewers create *parole* alongside Ritchie's vastly more complex and eloquent utterances in the drawings, paintings, and sculptures.

If just one principle could be cited as the heart of Ritchie's *langue*, it would have to be the second law of thermodynamics. The law states that every process that occurs in nature is irreversible and unidirectional, dictated by an overall increase in entropy. Entropy, which invades every system, is welcomed as a liberator into Ritchie's *langue*. Entropy is not anarchy, however. It exists in concert with the first law of thermodynamics, the conservation of energy. Even as the *langue* is transformed through entropy's beautiful havoc, its initial structure is still traceable.

The *parole* (the individual works) has undergone a parallel process of loosening up. No longer confined to straightforward;

no nonsense, factual statements, the *parole* has gone poetic, evocative rather than descriptive. It is in the intersection of these two moving targets—a shape—shifting *langue* with an entropic life of its own and *parole* that moves from "See Spot run" simplicity toward modernist poetry—that we can locate the source of the formal transformations in Ritchie's work since the late 1990s.

Drawings are the bedrock of most artists' practices, and Ritchie's project, based entirely on drawings, is no exception. The arc of the aesthetic that passes through *Proposition Player* on its way to an unknowable destination can be traced by comparing a key early series of drawings, *Autogenesis* (1997–98, figs. 28 and 29), with a later one, *Everyone Belongs to Everyone Else* (2001, fig. 30). *Autogenesis* comprises forty-nine small pencil and ink drawings on Mylar that closely parallel the forty-nine brief sections of a short story also called "Autogenesis," with the subtitle "Never start something you can't finish before you're dead," which was actually written a year after the drawings were made. To call the drawings illustrations isn't quite right, since that would seem to subjugate them to the story—if anything the short stories illustrate the drawings—but they do have illustrative qualities. Figures floating on blank fields, pulled out of space but not out of time, these sequential drawings narrate the story of the Big Bang through Ritchie's established avatars. In many of them, the angels/superheroes like Asta, Bubba, and Abbadon are perfectly recognizable as they perform their bit of the story.

XXXVI

Dokiel and Pistis Sophia; Judgment and Distribution, passed everything through the chiral mirror. Just to be sure.[1]

Drawing XXXVI shows Dokiel above with the scales of judgment and Pistis Sophia below holding an object made of rods with forms distributed along them. (The forms recall the wooden beads in *The God Game* (p. 116), which we will come to shortly.) Between the two figures is a shieldlike shape, presumably the chiral mirror, with forms flowing through it to the left and right.

XXXVII

The burnt out armor of the Future was hung on the mirror and time

assumed a one-way flow. Complex molecules evolved. Things were happening.*[2]

In the next drawing, Pistis Sophia has joined Dokiel at the top of the composition; they hold their icons together, with the burnt-out armor appended. Beneath them is a teeming mass of greenish tendrils dotted with reds—things are indeed happening.

XXXVIII

The universal genetic ancestor—Phul, the Royal Virus, emerged from the recoding of complex molecules. As it appeared, Raphael the Serpent king was dislodged from the City of Atoms, a palace coup. Everything changed as the map of atoms transcribed on to the map of biochemical processes... Twisting towers of protein with pilasters, balustrades and minarets growing from them, reach out to other towers, folding and coupling in a never ending ritual of exchange. Slick, purposeful motion is everywhere, everything is dissolving, building and twitching together in the rhythmic dance of biology.[3]

Silvery Phul and the yellow Serpent king appear in *Drawing XXXVIII*, separated by the towers and dancing biological forms that Ritchie describes.

Ritchie's "image language" in the *Autogenesis* drawings is nearly as precise as the written language in its pendant story. In these drawings, Ritchie's visual *parole* sticks close to his *langue*. He is now a native speaker of the tongue he has mothered who is taking pains to clearly describe a set of events unfolding over time, offering "Just the facts, ma'am." Viewers/readers can follow these closely, getting more than the gist and more than a satisfying impression of order. If they choose to tangle with his comically complex continuum—a completely optional choice, by the way, (and not for the faint of heart)—they are helped along by the graphite annotations that punctuate the images, annotations that also appear in his paintings and that form the bulk of his wall drawings.

Much has changed in the *Everyone Belongs...* suite of seven drawings made two years later. The drawings have grown a lot bigger, for one thing, and have slid to the far end of the time-space continuum. Rather than forty-nine sequential moments on 11 x 8-foot

TOP TO BOTTOM: FIG. 28 AND 29: *AUTOGENESIS XXXVI, XXXVII, AND XXXVIII* (1997–98). INK AND PENCIL ON MYLAR. 8 1/2 x 11 INCHES EACH (21.6 x 27.9 CM). COLLECTION OF HARRY W. AND MARY MARGARET ANDERSON

1. Matthew Ritchie, "Autogenesis," in *The Big Story* (Cleveland: Cleveland Center for Contemporary Art, 1999), p. 62.
2. Ibid, p. 62.
3. Ibid, p. 62.

sheets, these are seven places, or "climates" (a term Ritchie prefers), produced on large (22 x 65-inch) scrolls. As in Asian scrolls, many narrative moments happen at the same time in different areas of the image. The drawings are considerably looser than the *Autogenesis* drawings, with thin translucent washes that nearly reach the edges of the sheet. In the third drawing (fig. 30), a large body of water and a crescent-shaped beach stretch over the central section. A pair of figures walks along the beach at the upper left, passing a corpse. The water laps at small islands (or boats, or rocks, or a religious procession that is baptizing icons). Multicolored concentric ripples play over the water's surface, which is touched by thin rays of green and yellow light (or is it a pounding rain?). Strange shapes occupy the left side of the drawing: the dissolving form of the Swimmer, recognizable from other works, here labeled "MOTHER," and an unusual giant seedpod capped by a line drawing buzzing with many tiny yellow circles. Graphite glosses grace the whole surface, as they do in most of Ritchie's drawings and paintings, and include several equations and phrases like "The SHORE," "Solar energy" (near the buzzing lines), "beauty," and some illegible words and inscrutable squiggles, perhaps symbols, to the left of the pod. The edges of the crescent beach meet with warping planes, many of them red, a color

that usually signals time and entropy in Ritchiedom.

Although plenty of breathing space remains in the *Everybody Belongs…* compositions, they have lost the "small colored object on a large white field" quality of the early drawings that made them look like illustrations. The looser handling of colors and shapes corresponds directly to a looser handling of narrative. Here Ritchie has not provided play-by-play action in short story form, as he did in the earlier *Autogenesis* drawings. He has, however, provided a cryptic map in the 2002 *Games of Chance and Skill* catalogue produced by MIT (pp. 94–95). The corpse on the beach is "The Father Costume," the buzzing lines above the pod are "Lucifer's eyes," and the drowned Swimmer has already been noted. Some elements, like the large pod and the concentric ripples, are left unidentified.

Ritchie's visual language, straightforwardly descriptive in *Autogenesis*, has now become poetic and impressionistic. The formal vocabulary remains the same, but the grammar is loose and flexible, allowing the shapes and colors codified in *The Working Model* to pollute one another. This change in Ritchie's image-making parallels the transformation of modernity in literature from metonymy to metaphor, from linearity to simultaneity, from description to evocation. As entropy reshapes his *langue*, every utterance takes him and us to a new point of no return.

In Ritchie's paintings, this transition from prosaic to poetic is more pronounced. In *Lucky* (1998, fig. 31), beginning with the title, the artist hews closely to the body of information he has to convey. *Lucky* is one of Ritchie's original seven avatars, referencing Lucifer, free will, and light. His calling card is a pale blue color, prevalent on this canvas. One key detail, a pair of disembodied red hands pulling lines out from the exploding center, situates this image in the Function Suite of the Brockton Holiday Inn and/or (have it your way) the beginning of time, featured midway through the 1998 short story "The Gamblers." Our heroes have been trying to find their way out of the Function Suite and to get the Big Bang under way. To that end, they have gutted Bubba, representing the Planck Limit. Purson, the timekeeper, has just made his entrance:

When they came back in to the room, it was clear that Bubba wasn't going to be the end of it. Things were heating up too fast for that.

FIG. 30: *EVERYONE BELONGS TO EVERYONE ELSE* (THIRD DRAWING FROM SUITE OF SEVEN DRAWINGS), 2000–2001. INK AND GRAPHITE ON DENRIL. 22 x 65 INCHES (56 x 165 CM). THE MUSEUM OF MODERN ART, NEW YORK. PURCHASE. 02592.01.3

They were moving past the Planck Limit. Who knows what Lucky was thinking, high on crack, all sweated up from the killing? He made his move on the old guy as fast as anyone could but he was no match for a man made of time. The timekeeper's two hands, the hour and the minute, sneaked out faster than you could think, shuffled the cards, rolled the dice, grabbed Asta's coil of red wire and whipped it around Lucky's neck. Photons scattered as the superstrings cut through his throat in a perfect Schwarzschild radius, spraying over the couch, the carpet and the TV set, blurring the image of the cartoon show as the blood trickled down the screen.[4]

4. Matthew Ritchie, "The Gamblers," *Matthew Ritchie: Projects* (New York: Basilico Fine Arts, 1998), p. 39.

5. Matthew Ritchie, from "The Family Farm" in (*The World May Be*) *Fantastic*, Bienniale of Sydney (Melbourne: Bienniale of Sydney, 200), p. 182; and "The Big Story" in *The Big Story* (Cleveland: Cleveland Center for Contemporary Art, 1999), p. 62.

In the painting, Asta's red wire shatters like glass over the cloud-like figure of Lucky as he explodes outward into crystalline shapes colored in Bubba's pale green and gold. These color-coded tesserae, hallmarks of the early paintings and Sintra wallworks, are puzzle pieces. They convey the sense that everything fits together, everything is recombinant, everything clicks into place. Rest easy; the world (or more precisely the many worlds—gambling, Christianity, the Big Bang—that Ritchie stacks like layers in a cake and slices into paintings) makes sense.

Five years later, this reassuring clarity has melted into something more chaotic and true. *The Eighth Sea* (2003, p. 75) shares Lucky's central motif of a figure dissolving into space. The symbolic palette is also there, but it seems polluted compared to the Piero de la Francesca perfection of the earlier painting. Gone, too, is the opacity of the colors in the early work. This painting has thin translucent veils, light and shadow, sheaves of gossamer. The forms, like the colors, are polluted as well: geometric tesserae have been replaced by curves, vegetable shapes, and liquid shapes. Things are mushy and viscous where before they had been crystalline and dry. There is no clear-cut story to align with the picture. The following are quotes from writings that Ritchie proposed as descriptions of what's going on in *The Eighth Sea:*

Through it all, they carried their secret ocean inside them. The hidden sea that connects us all, whose tropical and sluggish tides ebb and flow through the caldera of the skull, trawling the shoals of memory, leaving driftwood carved in fantastic and familiar shapes.

A sea filled with iron, salt, and lust. You can't leave your blood behind.

Now that saline solution pounded in his head, yearning to return to its marine origins. His hands and feet flattened and fanned into ropes of flesh. His skin toughened and divided, his tattoos becoming rare and fantastic patterns. He felt his metabolism shift as the water that had been choking him became a sweet white air. For a moment, he felt the strangeness of his new body, reborn as a great blue star, and then even that dissolved into the infinite engine of ocean.[5]

The correlation between this painting and its text, compiled from fragments of other texts, is indirect, but it feels just as true as the earlier one. Although it may seem that Ritchie's descriptive system is less exact or scientific, in fact the opposite is the case. The more complex the descriptive system becomes, the more it looks exactly like that which it describes. The painting, like all the work in *Proposition Player*, moves closer to a one-to-one relationship with Ritchie's continuum, which is itself, through entropy's relentless fecundity, growing closer to the descriptive systems from which it initially departed. Like the emperor's map in Jorge Luis Borges' parable, covering reality, replacing it, and becoming its own reality, the work gets better at describing the world as it gets more complex. What looks

FIG. 31: *LUCKY*, 1998. OIL AND MARKER ON CANVAS, 80 x 200 INCHES (203 x 508 CM). COLLECTION RACHEL AND JEAN PIERRE LEHMANN

like sloshing, frothing chaos is in fact an increasingly complex order. The change from the reassuring clarity of *Lucky* to the bewildering shape-shifting in *The Eighth Sea* is from a falsely ordered system to an observed science, from something less scientific to something more scientific, though on the surface it appears that the reverse is true. Science, like language, transforms itself through its own capacity for incorporating change. Early (Aristotelian) science was perfect, but wrong. The perfect or ideal system is closed and dead. For a system to survive, it must bear entropy's slings and arrows.

Wall drawings anchor all of Ritchie's installations. These are done in black marker or with vinyl decals on walls painted in the artist's palette of high key blues, greens, and yellows. Looping arrows stitch together scientific equations, voodoo symbols, and phrases drawn from gambling. Whether crawling under a puzzle piece of Sintra and paintings or standing alone, they grow more complex over time. The infinite reproducibility and scalability of the wall drawings (they are traced on the walls from projections or cut from digital files), like the qualities of accessibility and interactivity, are of crucial importance to Ritchie's project. In fact, everything that Ritchie makes, including the paintings and texts, is iterative, but the wallworks are especially so. Iteration and scalability speak both to the rigor and to the flexibility of his continuum of ideas. What is true in a corner of one of the *Autogenesis* drawings from 1998 will be true in a giant sculpture of 2003, true across media and time. These qualities also speak to the essential thriftiness or conservatism of Ritchie's project: that which supports the Big Idea is conserved—as decreed by the first law of thermodynamics—that which doesn't is lopped off by Ockham's razor.

In *The Hierarchy Problem* (2003, pp. 14–15) for *Proposition Player*, all the drawings that Ritchie has done over the past seven years are reprised on the giant walls of the Contemporary Arts Museum Houston. But they have also slid off the walls and into open space in the form of a sculpture called *The Fine Constant* (2003, pp. 2,13–17). This work, comprising thirty-two 8 x 4-foot diecut aluminum plates come together to form a single drawing, emerges from the wall drawing to hover parallel to the floor. Together, *The Hierarchy Problem* and *The Fine Constant* establish X and Y axes that imply a Z: they describe a solid block of information space in

the gallery's huge volume. The equations, symbols, and lines in this imaginary block invisibly intertwine, breed, die, decay, and provide fertilizer for other forms in an orgy of entropy. Activating the whole volume of a space seems to have been Ritchie's intention with the wall drawings and the Sintra wallworks and floorworks all along.

Of all Ritchie's works—drawings, paintings, games, wallworks—perhaps the most telling pair of poles describing the continuing aesthetic transformations is *Working Model*, from 1995 and the deck of cards from 2003 (pp. 57–63), part of the game that is *Proposition Player*. The former is a seven by seven-unit grid that locks together much of Ritchie's initial source material with the avatars he created. This chart serves as a fairly reliable "super spy decoder ring" for those who feel compelled to get to the bottom of Ritchie's earliest installations. (The later installations are, in a manner of speaking, off the chart.) In the deck of cards, the grid's contents are remixed, altered, added to, and sprung free from the grid itself. A deck of cards implies shuffling, randomness, contradictory games, and innumerable winning and losing hands. All the hallmarks of Ritchie's *langue* are here: an open invitation to the viewer, the capacity to generate meaning on its own, the transformation wrought by entropy, and the conservation of earlier forms even as they are transformed.

Ritchie's project stretches between two fundamental and contradictory laws. By their decree, the quasi-language that he initially crafted, a crystalline esperanto drawn from physics and voodoo, metamorphosed into an ever-changing slang-filled pidgin, lively and unpredictable, perfect for the free verse riffs of *Proposition Player*. Ultimately, there can be no pidgin without riffs, or riffs without pidgin, just as there can be no drawings without context or context without drawings. These elements meld into a continuous whole without discernable divisions or parts, constantly transformed through a never ending cycle of exchange, through the call and response of information and energy, signal and noise, stasis and motion, conservation and entropy.

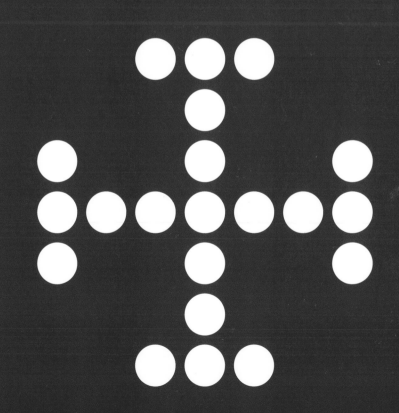

Illustrated Chronology

The texts and images in this section together reconstruct the central narrative in Matthew Ritchie's work from 1995–2003 leading up to *Proposition Player*.

EXPERIENCED TIME   INSTALLATION VIEW OF *EXPERIENCED TIME* IN "FABULISM," JOSLYN ART MUSEUM, OMAHA, NEBRASKA, 2004

AFTER THE FATHER COSTUME INSTALLATION VIEWS OF *AFTER THE FATHER COSTUME* AT C/O ATLE GERHARDSEN, BERLIN, 2003

THE BIG DOWN INSTALLATION VIEW OF *THE BIG DOWN* IN "PAINTING PICTURES," KUNSTMUSEUM WOLFSBURG, WOLFSBURG, GERMANY, 2003

AFTER LIVES   INSTALLATION VIEWS OF *AFTER LIVES* AT ANDREA ROSEN GALLERY, NEW YORK, 2002

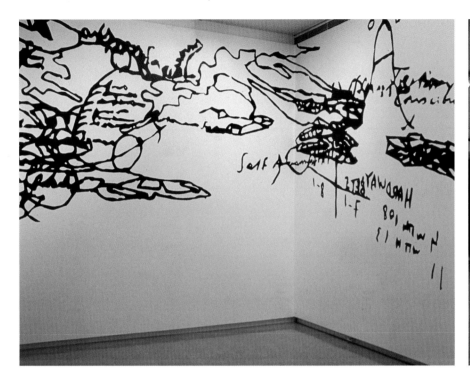

THE MAIN LINE   INSTALLATION VIEWS OF *THE MAIN LINE* IN "(THE WORLD MAY BE) FANTASTIC," BIENNIALE OF SYDNEY, SYDNEY, AUSTRALIA, 2002

GAMES OF CHANCE AND SKILL ABOVE AND OPPOSITE: INSTALLATION VIEWS OF *GAMES OF CHANCE AND SKILL*, PERMANENT INSTALLATION AT THE ALBERT AND BARRIE ZESIGER SPORTS AND FITNESS CENTER, MASSACHUSETTS INSTITUTE OF TECHNOLOGY, CAMBRIDGE, MASSACHUSETTS, 2002

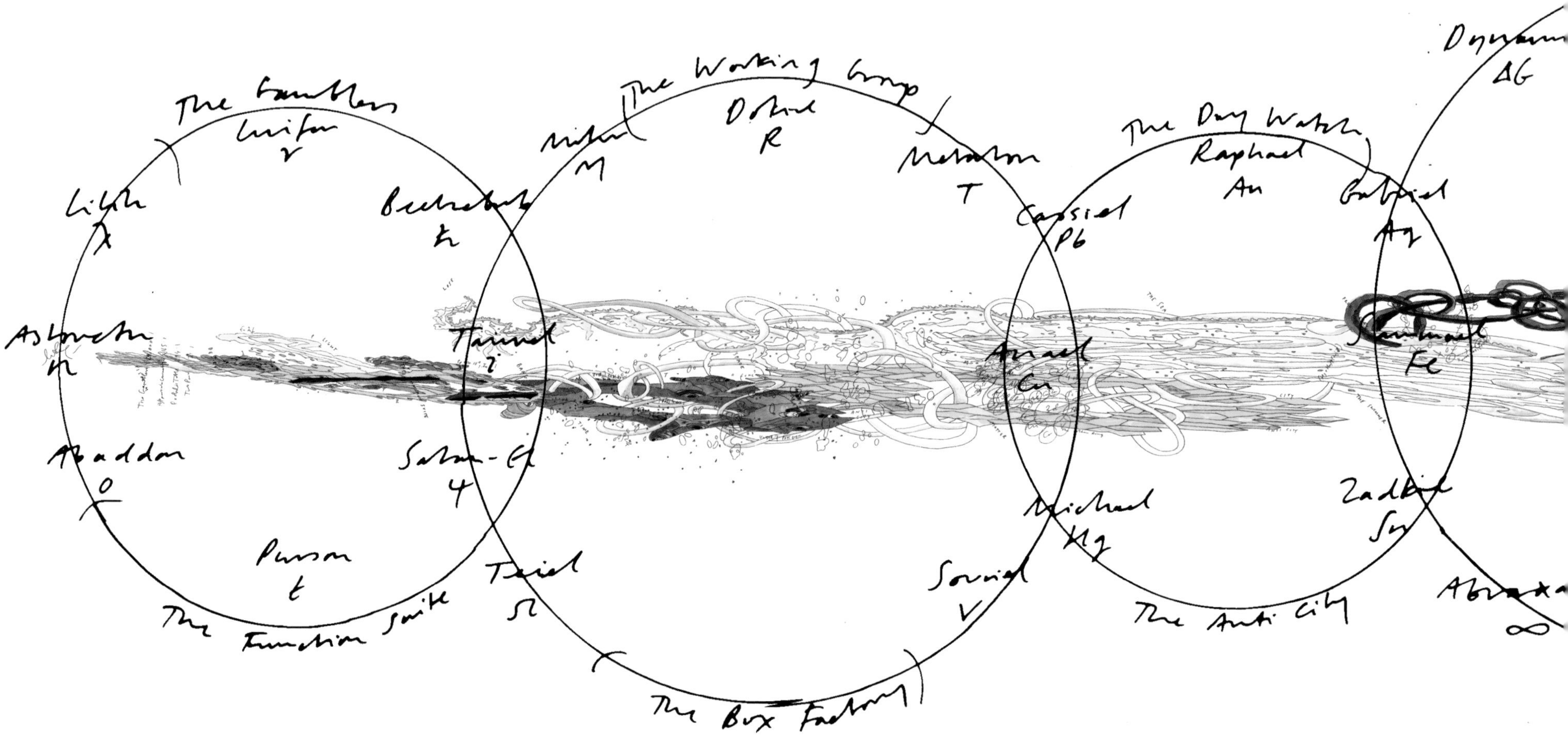

The Gamblers
Lucifer
r

Lilith
x

Astorath
th

Abaddon
0

Person
t

The Function Suite

Beelzebub
Bz

Hanniel
i

Sabnum-El
4

Tziel
N

The Working Group

Mihr
M

Oshie
R

Metatron
T

Cassiel
P6

Azrael
Cu

Michael
Hg

Sarviel
V

The Box Factory

The Day Watch
Raphael
Au

Gabriel
Ag

Zadkiel
Sn

The Anti City

Dayenu
AG

Shamael
Fe

Abraxas
∞

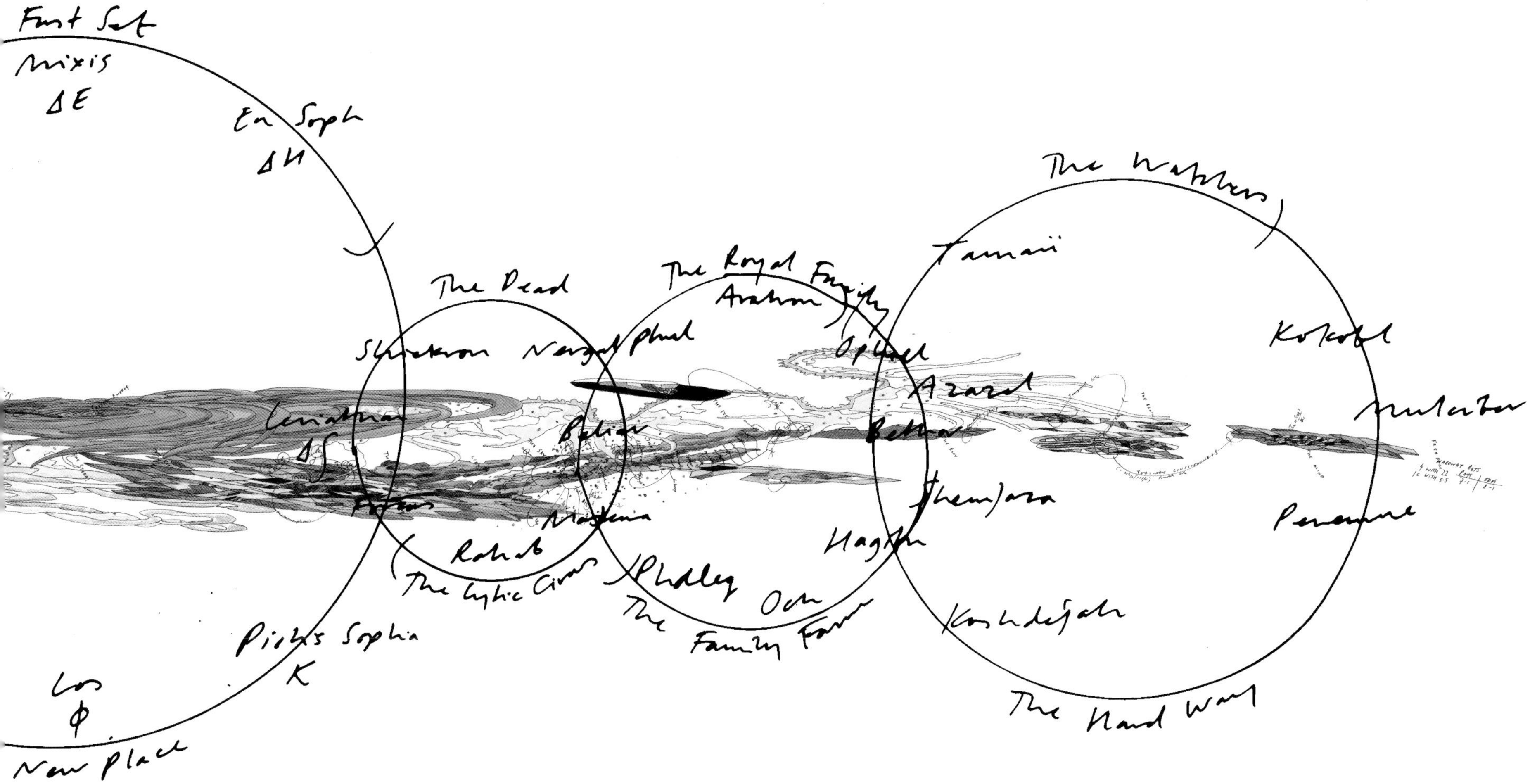

First Set
mixis
ΔE

En Soph
ΔH

The Watchers

The Dead
The Royal Family
Tamai

Arakim

Kokobi

Shekarron Nargat Phul
Optiel
nulcator

Azazel

Leviathan
Bebion
Bethron

Peranml

Pistos
Shemjaza

Masfenu

Haghm

Robab
Koshdejah

The Lyric Circus
Phalley Och

Piotis Sophia
K
The Family Farm

cos
φ
The Hard Way

New Place

Jenelle Porter

Five Percent More

In the new universe of subatomic particles, for example, scientists have identified twelve different varieties of the quark… which are distinguished by six flavors, three colors, three anti-colors, and varying degrees of "strangeness." Chance, random order, and game playing, those familiar tools of the contemporary artist, have invaded scientific methodology….[1]

Over the last several years Matthew Ritchie's art work has explored and documented the manifold creation myths of the universe: religious, scientific, and mythological. Though it employs traditional practices of painting, sculpture, and drawing, Ritchie's work extends to nontraditional installations that incorporate enormous light boxes, vinyl and pen wall drawings, books, and website projects. Short stories, written to accompany each body of work, reference pulp fiction, voodoo, folklore, and mythology, and cover topics ranging from love, horror, sex, and loss to gambling, quantum physics, religion, and moral consequences (among other things). Ritchie distills these varied elements until they are compressed to their simplest form: information. For him, information is raw material to be dizzyingly mapped and diagrammed across and through his systems of color, line, paint, metal, glass, and light. Just as Joseph Beuys mapped the "amorphous stuff of life" to delineate a desired clarity, Ritchie's iconographic gestures prescribe an analytical study of how information arranges itself in a closed system. Here, the system just happens to be a model of the formation of the universe.

In a general sense, Ritchie's works present the universe as a metaphorical shape colonized by embodiments of Creation's talking points. This story, an intricate one to be sure, is inhabited by forty-nine characters who occupy various space-time situations and represent fundamental structures and laws of science. Collectively, they possess multitudinous characteristics that collapse onto one another like a telescoping rod. They are an illustrious and profane bunch: complicated, desirous, violent, gorgeously alluring; both profoundly romantic and deeply cynical.[2] Each character has a name (indeed multiple names) and attributes drawn from opposing and even self-canceling traditions of science and faith. Although

1. Calvin Tomkins, *Duchamp: A Biography* (New York: Henry Holt and Company, Inc., 1996), p. 444.
2. Here, the word cynical references cynicism's ancient Greek origins as a philosophical sect founded by Antisthenes, a pupil of Socrates. Originally, cynicism embodied a radical idealism, albeit one that extolled a theory of eroded faith in human sincerity. The true cynic renounced human comforts for extreme asceticism. With this in mind, contemporary cynicism can be interpreted as an incomplete project, a failure of nerve to transcend the limits of society.

the characters reflect their specific sources, they constantly morph and mutate through parallel and overlapping timelines, embodying competing beliefs and theorems that subsequently elide all such oppositions. In other words, they cancel one another out, as abstraction and figuration, fact and fiction, fuse into something greater than the sum of their parts. At the end of this colossal story there will be a single remaining character, a personage who contains all the other characters along with their respective intricacies in a single schizophrenic bundle of energy and mass. In other words, a final player.

In 2002 Matthew Ritchie created a permanent, site-specific piece for the Massachusetts Institute of Technology (MIT)[3]. This installation, *Games of Chance and Skill*, tinkered with the relationships among history, matter, and consciousness, gathering all of Ritchie's cosmogonies in one place for the first and perhaps only time. The images from the MIT installation (pp. 92–95, 100) can be used as a key to this compendium and as an illustrated guide to this essay.

One component of *Games of Chance and Skill* is an eighty-foot long plane of brightly colored forms overlaid with chaotic fragments and equations that restate the actions taking place inside the forms. It is graffitied with its own scientific and allegorical meanings. Fundamental equations of scientific theory—Einstein's General Theory of Relativity, Shannon's information equations,[4] the laws of thermodynamics, and the Yang-Mills equation[5]—mingle with notations ranging from gambling odds and voodoo symbols to angelic seals from ceremonial magic. The collection of marks represents how an idea, an object, and a place can overlap. For example, when we read a scientific equation, such as H_2O, we immediately think of, and possibly see and feel, water. Ritchie's notations, which are guides for himself as much as for the viewer, provide written clues to the diagram's larger narrative.

The diagram "reads" from left to right, from right to left, or from both sides simultaneously. It also reads through and into Ritchie's entire oeuvre, including his various short stories. This explanatory essay attempts to do the same, referring to material both abstract and literal as it describes the shapes, legends, and colors that signify the "heroes" and the "villains" in this story. Let's begin.

On the far left, the gray branching shape represents Astoreth, a character whose attribute is number ("n"), the first unknown quantity, the first coordinate. Here, even at the start, things get tricky and begin to shape-shift. Astoreth (an ancient figure from Persian mythology), or Asta, is a hermaphrodite, willing and able to play it both ways. Asta is the lover of Stanley, a one-eyed cardsharp also known as Satan-el, whose defining attribute is duality. In modern science, duality is represented by the Greek letter ψ, a symbol that was once termed the "devil's trident." Originally, Satan-el (or just plain old Satan, as he's known these days) was the moniker given to the angel chosen to defend human souls in the high court of heaven. (Satan-el literally means "adversary of God," and it was by no means considered a dishonorable title.) So he's an angel and a defense attorney, a situation riddled with clichés in a grim, pitiable way.

The introduction of these first two characters, fraught as they are with theological and ethical levels of meaning, establishes the synchronic proposal of Ritchie's epic. The relationship between number and duality, between Astoreth and Satan-el, perhaps best represents an assumption the artist seeks to dismantle: the either/ or intricacies of history, religion, and consciousness. Even with only two characters in play, multiple forms of representation, not to mention an unstable web of coincidence, are introduced along with proposals of origin and outcome.

Astoreth and Satan-el are members of the Gamblers, one of seven families of characters signifying competing theological positions.[6] Each family has seven members representing differing sexual, functional, and ethical orientations within the group. A color assigned to each member often serves as an oblique link between generations and timelines. Each family occupies a specific place and phase in the timeline of the universe. The Gamblers, for example, occupy the Function Room, a place somewhere out there in time but physically located geographically at the seedy Brockton Holiday Inn just outside Boston on Route 24. They have hard-core drug and gambling problems—they're high stakes all the way around. Their cause célèbre is randomness. They are simultaneously the moment before the Big Bang and the spark that ignites it.

The remaining five Gamblers round out the initial conditions of the universe. The green mass is Lilith (Frequency), and the arm of soft blue funneling aloft is Lucifer (Light), or Lucky. The black represents Abaddon, or Zero, inverse twin and brother to Asta. Here,

3. The permanent installation, *Games of Chance and Skill* (2002), was commissioned for the recently opened Albert and Barrie Zesiger Sports and Fitness Center on the MIT campus in Cambridge, Massachusetts. The eighty-foot-long, site-specific commission consists of a mosaic wall piece, a ceiling light box, and an etched-glass window.
4. Claude Elwood Shannon (1916–2001) pioneered mathematical communication theory, which led to information theory.
5. Named after theorists Chen Yang and Robert Mills, this set of field equations describes the strong force that holds atoms together. It became the basis for the electroweak theory and the study of quantum chromodynamics, which in turn contributed to the search for the so-called unified theory in physics.
6. The story of the Gamblers was first exhibited in several locations in 1998, including Basilico Fine Arts, New York; Mario Diacono Gallery, Boston; and Galeria Camargo Vilaca, São Paulo; the families themselves were first mapped out in a schematic exhibition titled *Working Model* at Basilico Fine Arts in 1995.

before space and time, we find the swapping of fermions (subatomic particles/the stuff) and bosons (subatomic particles/the energy) that characterizes the earliest state of the known universe. When we arrive at the edge of this phase, portrayed by a jagged, yellow ellipse, the real action begins. The yellow ring is Bubba, a.k.a. Beelzebub, who is eviscerated by the other Gamblers in the hotel room. This evil deed represents accelerated quantum decoherence. The rupture of the yellow circle in Ritchie's visual schema is your basic Big Bang. Shortly after Bubba's disembowelment, Purson (the Timekeeper and the seventh Gambler) shows up and carries away Lucifer's decapitated head, lopped off in retaliation for Bubba's murder. This action represents the integration of energy, light, material, and time ($E=mc^2$), or as Ritchie states, the basic conditions necessary for art making.

After this rather disturbing first act, more and more characters emerge. The large red circle is the period just after the Big Bang, the first million years when matter became intermingled with energy. Some say that this was the locus for the formation and distribution of linear time; others disagree. In this (cosmologically) brief moment, everything is still in play. The red disk is also the millstone that the angel Dokiel (a.k.a. Duke) will throw into the waters of the world at the end of time. So time contains its demise at its very conception. Hold onto that one.

At this moment in time, the red circle is inhabited by an assembly of angels called the Working Group.[7] They work in the Box Factory, a metaphorical place where the early universe is constructed. By day they organize the universe, giving it shape. They personify the basic properties of matter—volume, temperature, and mass—matched with mathematical indices of possibility and chance. After hours, they're members of a rock band, though they're really only in it for the rock-star outfits. Metatron (Temperature) wears a circa 1975 Bootsy Collins pantsuit emblazoned with stars, the uniform from Parliament's "Funkadelic" tour. Mihr (Mass) dons rapper Missy Elliot's bubble suit, a huge "M" plastered to the chest. Teiel, not an angel so much as a futuristic robot, wears Yohji Yamamoto from David Bowie's 1973 "Aladdin Sane" tour. Omael (the Index of atomic species) is outfitted in a bejeweled 1967 Profils du Monde dress created for Michelle Phillips of The Mamas and the Papas. Souriel (Volume) parades a

sexy Isaac Hayes cape. Tamuel (the Angel of Chance) wears a Zandra Rhodes tunic designed for Roger Taylor of Queen. Last, but not least, is Dokiel (distribution R) in his red, Sgt. Pepper-era Beatles suit. The hideous polyphony of musical styles that this group produces can only be Kepler's music of the spheres, a dissonant din based on a flawed geometric model of the solar system.[8]

The yellow crystalline ring that follows the red circle is the circle of hydrogen, the first element, which will fuel the stars. Unfolding orbits form a city composed of 109 polygonal segments, one for each element of the periodic table. This city is occupied by the Day Watch, a police force composed of the seven Archangels of yore. The first three appear (in a parallel timeline that corresponds to that of the Gamblers), in a horror story titled "The Bad Need."[9] Anael (Copper), or Anna Elizardo, a police detective, works with Michael (Mercury), a.k.a. Mike "The Lion" Di Angelis, her aging and slippery partner, and Sammael (Iron), a.k.a. Sam Morden, a very, very bad cop indeed (Sammael is traditionally the angel of death). Anna, Mike, and Sam investigate a ritual murder that has taken place in a high-rise office building. They find the victims eviscerated and arranged in a voodoo vévé, with entrails, blood, and shit drawing out the intricate patterns.[10] This horrific scene is the work of Scheikron, a demonic personality and an infection from another family. The remaining Archangels, Gabriel, Raphael, Zadkiel, and Cassiel, do not appear until "The Iron City," the sequel to "The Bad Need." These Archangels of the Day Watch represent the theological dream of absolute order, the fantasy of universal control. They, like all of Ritchie's characters, will find their particular brand of monomania profoundly challenged.

"The City" in the diagram mirrors and is generated by its counterpart, the Anti-City. This is where the Archangels of the Day Watch first encounter their oppositional family, The Dead: prison inmates recently escaped from the Lytic Circus, a gigantic and allegedly perfectly designed prison that looms outside the City. The prison refuses to admit its institutional failures and so classifies the six escapees—Belphegor (Adsorption), Forcas (Lysis), Mastema (Transcription), Nergal (Substitution), Rahab (Replication), and Scheikron (Infection)—as not missing but dead. They too will appear in "The Iron City."

The Dead articulate the life cycle of a virus, the culmination of which is lysis: the rupture of the host cell. Technically, a virus is

7. "The Working Group" was exhibited in 1999 at c/o Atle Gerhardsen, Oslo.
8. Johannes Kepler (1571–1630) was a German astronomer with one foot in science and the other in medievalism. He discovered the laws governing planetary motion, but also promoted the notion that the planets created music.
9. Published by Parkett Editions in 2001.
10. In voodoo ceremonies, a vévé is a ceremonial design, representing astral forces, drawn upon an object or the grounds of a temple. See excerpt from *Secrets of Voodoo* in this catalogue, p. 125.

nonbiotic (dead) genetic material that relies on a live host in order to reproduce. The struggle between the Day Watch and the Dead that occurs in "The Bad Need" is more than just a metaphor for order versus chaos, or life and death—it is about the sterility of an ordered, ruled state in contrast to the potential complexity of an anarchic, but vital, existence.

The seventh character of The Dead, Beliar (Transmission), may or may not be the adult offspring of the Astronaut and the Actress, whose stories are told in "The Fast Set" and "The Slow Tide." All three stories are concerned with building a larger conceptual area: "The New Place."[11] The New Place is an area of the story that precedes, encompasses, and survives the struggles of the characters in "The Bad Need," and its prequels, "The Fast Set," and "The Slow Tide." It is the earth, the newest place in the universe.

The New Place is primarily defined by a large sky, a sinuous blue and gray shape identified as "The Swimmer." This is the headless corpse of Lucifer, decapitated at the Holiday Inn, now fused with Asta to form Abraxas (Infinity). Mantled by the fringe of Bubba's yellow gut, the Swimmer is the visible universe, the world of light, the known stars and galaxies. "The Fast Set" story line, floating as it does between 1937 and 1963, encapsulates the history of thermodynamics as seen through Gnostic mythology.[12]

In "The Slow Tide," the Swimmer manifests as Emmett, a senile bodybuilder who ultimately drowns in a freak storm off the coast of South Florida. But before this ending, we are introduced to a much younger Emmett, in 1938, as he experiences a drug-induced hallucination presided over by Mlle. Florida (Pistis Sophia), a voodoo loa imaged by white, free-floating circles. In Gnosticism, she represents the property of wisdom or balance; thermodynamically, she is equilibrium. We learn as well that *emet* is the Hebrew word for truth, and its inscription on the forehead of a golem will activate it. So of course we need a golem, and that would be Morris.

Flash forward to 1963, the beginning of the space age. Morris, or Los as he's known in Gnosticism, represents labor. He waits deep below Miami Beach's luxurious Eden Roc hotel, paralyzed and petrified like the calcified coccoliths that make up the area's coastal reefs. The Golem is in love with the redheaded Actress (Mixis), our tragic heroine. His body, formed of crystals, geodes, and magne-

tites, is like a massive reception antenna: images of, and words about, the Actress are transmitted directly into his soul. Morris pines for her, awaiting the day when he can possess her.

The Actress, as in any twisted love triangle, loves another: the Sky Boy. The brown curlicues in the drawing are free energy, the trail of the Sky Boy, a.k.a. Dynamis, or the Astronaut. (It may well turn out that the senile bodybuilder is the father of the Astronaut.) Morris' longing disrupts the electromagnetic system, which causes the Astronaut's mission to go haywire, and he flies into the heart of an angry green tornado (system energy). The overlapping brown (Dynamis) and green (Mixis) masses represent the union of free energy and system energy, the liaison between the Astronaut and the Actress. Their offspring, a golden baby, conceived at the climax of the storm that drowns Emmett, is enthalpy.

In "The Slow Tide" most of the characters disappear. The Golem, the Actress, Mlle. Florida, the Swimmer, and the Astronaut are all absorbed into their environments. But the infinite blue in which the millstone sinks is a different kind of ocean, now incorporated with the body of the Bodybuilder/Swimmer. In Ritchie's work, the integration of character and place, as this story shows, marks the end of a particular phase. As noted above, the seven characters of the Fast Set and "The Slow Tide" derive from Gnosticism, an esoteric doctrine that seeks to make sense of the obvious physical problems of the visible universe by blaming its actual construction on a malevolent demiurge. In a grander sense, it is an attempt to deal with the problem of death. In scientific terms, death is interpreted through the second law of thermodynamics which articulates the rule that any form of work, such as living, will result in a net transfer of energy away from the working system. In other words, life's a bitch and then you die. The loss of energy over time is called entropy, and it is the defining principle of the experienced universe.

Throughout the stories and the works themselves, red shapes signal the ultimate instability of any thermodynamic system: the Golem hears the red snakes of entropy following him; red references the skin color of the Timekeeper; and it is the color of Officer Sam Morden's hair. As Emmett drowns in 1963, a red flower blooms in his heart—a red flower that blooms gruesomely again in 2001 in "The Bad Need." Finally, Dokiel will throw that red millstone into the

11. "The New Place" web project was commissioned by the San Francisco Museum of Modern Art in 2001.
12. This story was first told in a large exhibition at the Museum of Contemporary Art, North Miami, Florida, in 2000, and concluded as "The Slow Tide," at the Dallas Museum of Art in 2001.

waters of the world at the end of time. Put simply, when you see red, you are in the presence of death.

Finally, the combined narrative activities of The Fast Set, the Day Watch, and the Dead generate and complete the firm ground of the New Place, the location of the rest of the stories, a place where thermodynamics, chemistry, and prebiotic molecules form the basis for the evolution of life.[13] As illustrated in the painting *Germinal* (p. 74), and in *Games of Chance and Skill*, a columnar green shape slanting up from the brown mass indicates the Tree of Life. It grows on the Family Farm, a place worked by members of the Royal Family, who symbolize the seven kingdoms of life. Phul, the viral king, dismantles the periodic table of the City, turning atoms into life. He's the bridge to and from the viral kingdom where the familiar kingdoms of life evolve: Ophiel (Monera) is the bacterial kingdom; Hagith (Protista), the kingdom of multicellular organisms; Och (Plantae), the plant kingdom; Bethor (Animalia), the animal kingdom; Phaleg (Fungi) the fungal kingdom; and, Aratron (Archaea), the first kingdom of life, the first step in evolution. The kingdoms of life share one fundamental quality: they are mortal.

Named after the seven Olympic Spirits of ceremonial magic, the Royal Family characters turn Gnosticism on its ear. Although from one position the universe can be perceived as flawed, from another defects are its greatest asset. Imperfection allows opportunities for growth, adaptation, and change. The Royal Family's parallel story is one of family secrets, missing children, and multigenerational conspiracy. Significantly, one of the Royals owns a company housed in the Meitner building, the very same company that employed the massacre victims of "The Bad Need."

The Tree of Life grows on and up to the forms of the Watchers, illuminated as part of "The Hard Way," the first chapter in Ritchie's atemporal saga.[14] The Watchers' story derives from one of the books of the Apocrypha, and is a Promethean tale of angels who bring knowledge to humanity and are punished for the offense.[15] The daughters of Cain went out and got with these nasty angels, the rebel Watchers, which of course leads to a whole host of other complications. In another timeline, the Watchers are a group of itinerant hippies who occupy the Hard Way, a 2,000-year-old road that runs through the middle of England. They not only trigger the

last ice age, but also fall to earth at its end, one to each of the seven continents, accelerating the creation of modern humankind.

From the branches of the Family Farm's Tree of Life sprout irregular, variously hued shapes that represent the seven lobes of the brain, which correspond to the Watchers. Yellow is an abstracted limbic system, the part of the brain concerned with basic emotions and instinctive actions. It is home to Shemjaza who, like his ancestor Bubba, will be dismembered. Red is the medulla oblongata (sensual and entropic appetites), the mushy part of the brain connected to the spinal cord. This is Azazel, the hoariest and most popular of demons and leader of the Watchers. Blue is the cerebellum, home to Kashdejah. Tamaii is the black shape, the occipital nerve (sight). The white bisected brain is Kokabel, the parietal lobe (memory and sensory functions), and gray is Penemue, a.k.a. Penny, the temporal lobe (time and space). Floating off to the far right is a green form, the frontal lobe, home to Mulciber the Builder—the first and last of Ritchie's characters. At last glance, the Watchers were camping out in the abandoned Family Farm and digging through its secrets.

Although enormously complex, this grand story is not a collection of mystic truths to be revealed or lessons to be learned. Ritchie resists the compulsion to avoid the difficult in art, and his interest in complexity extends far beyond the creation of a personal cosmogony. The often contradictory information featured in his work is drawn from our own strange human history and its telling is an act of generosity, a sharing of collective knowledge, a tall tale told around the fire. It is a story of how primal causes and irredeemable effects are automatically interpreted through the perspective of our own local concerns.

Scientists posit that we can account for only five percent of the universe; if we open our eyes wide, Ritchie's work allows us perhaps five percent more of the big picture, to see more of what surrounds us. Ritchie gives us some powerful tools for understanding the origins of the universe, one of the most difficult concepts we might ever wrap our brains around. Yet the documents created by his vast project are as much about incompleteness as they are about completeness. We propose that you use this color-coded map of creation as a key to deciphering the universe—a version of a version with vivid characters to cheer for and hiss at. This is just one way to tell it, and as Ritchie says, everything is true—except for the parts he made up.

13. *Parents and Children*, was exhibited at Andrea Rosen Gallery, New York, in 2000. *The Family Farm*, was shown at White Cube, London, in 2001.
14. *The Hard Way* was exhibited at galleries in Paris, New York and Oslo in 1998.
15. The Book of the Watchers was written by the prophet Enoch around the second century B.C. In Judeo-Christian myth, Enoch is the only man to turn into an angel: he becomes Metatron (also a character from the Working Group in Ritchie's cosmography). In the fourth century A.D., the books of the Apocrypha were excised from the Bible by the Council of Nicea.

An earlier version of this text was published in *Matthew Ritchie: Incomplete Projects 05* (Cambridge: Massachusetts Institute of Technology, 2003). The information herein was gleaned from countless conversations and correspondences with the artist. He is obviously the expert on the intricacies of his own work, and I thank him for his invaluable and extensive contributions.

GAMES OF CHANCE AND SKILL   *GAMES OF CHANCE AND SKILL* (DETAIL), 2002. PERMANENT INSTALLATION AT THE ALBERT AND BARRIE ZESIGER SPORTS AND FITNESS CENTER, MASSACHUSETTS INSTITUTE OF TECHNOLOGY, CAMBRIDGE, MASSACHUSETTS

Matthew Ritchie

The Bad Need

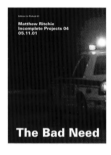

Anna stands stock still, not daring to move, unable to look at what is in the room. Through the panoramic windows, the lights of the old Lanthan factories are visible across the river, still outgassing clouds of poisonous steam from the infernal processes they use to make dog food, or whatever they make out there. She gazes blindly out into the blackness. But no matter how long she stares, the shadows pooling in the room eclipse the world of night outside. Her eyes turn into black sky. Di Angelis is openly sobbing, tears of humiliation for a lost world, whose psychic bargains have suddenly stretched far beyond his means. So much for "the Lion." She looks over to Morden and the fucker has his tight little smile strapped on, snug as a leather belt. He's actually turned on by this carnage, this madness. He catches her eye and traps it with his terrible gaze. His pupils are dilated, the bloom of the iris opening up, sucking her into his predator's dream. She can read his mind across the room.

"This is where I come from," he's thinking, "this is where we cross the line together. Out in to the night." He winks at her, the gesture binding her as a co-conspirator, an alloy, a future lover. Her eyes dart away and many faces, scattered as blank and serene as cut flowers, look back. A line of text scrawled in blood across the wall, stands out. "Prepare yourself for a big surprise and then, an even bigger surprise." She's suffocating, her lungs are are filling up, she's drowning in a sea of blood. The smells of death, excrement, and desire fuse with the scent of rotten bananas and the taste of the sea. She stumbles back out of the door and vomits.

"Screw you," she thinks; meaning Morden, the room full of blood and night, herself....

... It was a crime scene like no other. The remains had been carefully arranged in a rough circle round the room, nervous systems, tendons, intestines and bones, meticulously deployed to pick out an intricate radial form whose finer details were articulated with blood and shit. Impenetrable slogans and cryptic signs decorated the walls and windows. It was a provocation, a ritualized multiple murder squared and cubed. It was the past, long thought dead and buried, come courting. It was what lay behind the past, ancient memories of blood and the sea, come back to seek their center.

If you were a doctor, used to the abstract structures and extraordinary reactions hidden under the skin, you might be impressed by the thoroughness with which substantial alterations had been made to what had once been human beings, who are fairly resilient even in death. If you were an art critic, you might remark on the scene's passing resemblance to the work of certain contemporary artists and filmmakers, eager to capitalize on the shock value of death and dismemberment. If you were a historian, you would know that the tiny log cabin outside city hall was erected on the site of a scene exactly like this one. You would recall stories of a morning as smooth and clean as a new axe handle and the sound of screams in a silver storm. If you were a fortune teller, you would see the seeds of a future clotted with uncertainty, as ciphers of life and death tumbled from the cards. The anti-city, remembering itself.

But these were not doctors, critics, historians or fortune tellers. They were just policemen and women, ordinary people who'd seen enough violence and sorrow. As they stood there, miserable and frustrated, the murders slowly filled them, one by one, with a righteous anger, a shared hatred that crossed all the tired lines of sex, race, age and rank. From the night commander to the crime scene investigators, detectives and patrolmen, they caught light from a flame set by a pyromaniac. They could see plainly now just what they were up against. Disease polluted the civic body. A virus had announced itself with the clarity of a train full of Ebola victims turning up at central station. It was a bad thing: the bad thing that you couldn't run away from, couldn't rehabilitate, couldn't wait for it to "get better." No measure was too extreme to combat this corrosion before it penetrated to the core, even as the skin oxidized and flaked away to rust and air. They were all Mordens now, an Iron Precinct. In the days and years to come, they would stoke the department with their rage until it became a furnace of purity, searing the city, torching the streets clean, until the night burned as brightly and as cleanly as the day.

But they were just fuel to the fire, fuel to the fire.

THE FAMILY FARM   ABOVE AND OPPOSITE: INSTALLATION VIEWS OF *THE FAMILY FARM* AT WHITE CUBE, LONDON, 2001

Matthew Ritchie

The Slow Tide

Water. From the slate gray tides of the North Sea to the carmine canals of your arteries, inching forward in sapphire glaciers and carving furrows in solid black rock, water builds and dissolves, lifting up cathedrals of flesh and eroding mountains all at once, in a mad boiling race with no end. Whether it's a light evening rain in Paris or an endless monsoon in Thailand, whether it's coffee or Coke: from the hydraulics of your muscles to the saliva in your mouth, water drenches the world, saturates it, transforms it. How can we call it Earth? When it is a world made meaningful, brought to life by water.

Emmett stood on the beach and looked at all that water.

Back in the long day of the twentieth century, he'd been one of the original "fast men" in the golden age of silent comedy. With outrageous dexterity, he and his brothers in that lost fraternity had clambered along the roofs of rattling trains and skipped across the canvas wings of tilting aeroplanes, swung like monkeys on tilting ladders and gigantic clocks, juggled bricks, custard pies and ballpeen hammers with equal ease.

Later, people would imagine the impossible speed of those stunts to be some quaint leftover from the childhood of movies. But they really were faster, moving from frame to frame too quickly for film to capture. They were a fraternity, a questing order of clowns whose grail was the smoother trip, the maximum unsustainable load, the ultimate pratfall. Captured on film, they were time and space chopped into a chain of fragments from a fluid sequence of perfect, improbable risks....

…Emmett was on his way back to shore when the storm climbed down the pressure gradient to disaster. He felt its presence first as a light rain, pleasantly cool on his scalp and shoulders in the hot afternoon sun. After a few minutes, the speed of the rain increased, whipping the surface into thousands of tiny wavelets. He turned around slowly in the warm water and stopped swimming, breathing quietly, treading water lightly, as above him he saw the great wheel starting to turn in the sky. The air was humming, spokes of unseen electrical energy radiating from the center of the storm, whipping through the afternoon sky to caress the foam. The sea wind stank of ozone and

imminent death. The waves began to crest and fall more deeply. He could feel the deep pulse of the ocean underneath him....

…He gave it a good shot, you have to say that much. He took all those years catching beer bottles and buckets of paint, jumping though doors and rolling out of moving automobiles and forced them into this simple, endless moment of breathing, movement and breathing. The secret of the fast men was that the universe is what you understand it to be. If time appears to be moving slowly you are moving fast. For a moment he was fast again, swimming in a tight crawl, chopping through the whitecaps like a dolphin on crystal meth. Grunting, arcing and diving, arms as light as sails, hands like riverboat paddles; he was unstoppable. Outside space, faster than time, he could turn the years into seconds, the miles ahead into inches. He was a magician, he could turn the ocean into land. He would reach the shore in minutes, if he could only…

You can't beat the clock.

The waves caught him and rolled him, smacked him down, turned him again. As the green storm blossomed above, in its garden of water and air, a matching red orchid bloomed deep inside his aged heart. This was no box-car to be outmaneuvered, no pie to dodge; speed is irrelevant to an infinitely standing wave. The saline solution of his blood pounded in his head, yearning to return to its marine origins. There was a rushing noise as the soft jelly of his brain smashed against his skull as he went under for the last time. He caught the scent of flowers and powdered seashells, mixed with the iron of his blood. The storm receded above him and he sank soundlessly into the big down, drifting in a world without division, without boundary.

THE SLOW TIDE

ABOVE AND BOTTOM RIGHT: INSTALLATION VIEWS, *THE SLOW TIDE*, IN *CONCENTRATIONS 38: MATTHEW RITCHIE*, THE DALLAS MUSEUM OF ART, 2000

BOTTOM LEFT: *BIG TOP* (DETAIL), 2000. OIL AND MARKER ON CANVAS. 84 x 96 INCHES (213 x 244 CM)

Matthew Ritchie

The Fast Set

When he said goodbye at last, she just stood there in the twilight and frowned in an absent-minded sort of way. He knew that she was trying hard to figure out how to be truly herself in this awful and banal moment. And after a time she came up for air with a smile made all out of white teeth, lined up neatly like tombstones. It said, "whether you come back or not, I'll never see you again."

Not so much later he climbed into his Corvette and roared off, on his way across the state to the bars in Cocoa Beach and one last rat-race with the boys. Tomorrow he would drive over to the Cape where the future was waiting, pointed up at the sky like a billion dollar bullet. . . .

The astronaut had met her three months before his flight, at a reception for the Reverend King being held down in Miami. The first black astronaut, the visionary, and the famous actress, on a stage out by the pool, posing together in that fantastically ostentatious building, almost a film set in itself really. It was an incredible moment, outrageously glamorous, as the royalty of celebrity, power and danger mingled under the spotlights and the flash bulbs.

She looked perfect to him, as good as the movies, even with all the makeup and the teased and lacquered hair. Even though she was white, so translucently white she almost glowed pale green, fluorescing like some exotic metal burning under the lights, her famous red hair glittering with a thousand shades of desire, with a million flames of entropy and peril. She wore the green dress that night. That dress, with the folded twist of cloth at the base of the neck in the shape of a flower, a whirlpool, a storm, a strange attractor. The dress she would die in.

And deep in his labyrinth beneath the fabulously vulgar hotel, Morris the Golem was watching them that evening, on closed circuit television, his eyes on her, only her. Below him in the service tunnels he could hear the snakes turning in the red night of their fathomless desire. An odd kind of scratchy, slithery sound like the end of an old record, the static you hear when time runs out. He could always hear them, anytime, night or day, wherever he was. . . .

Over the centuries he had excavated endlessly, fearlessly. He had found wonders down there: caverns cut from solid diamond, lakes of burning pitch, a hidden lapidary world far below the surface of the earth. He carved an underground city from the soft white rock,

skyscrapers in negative space, parks of carefully tended fungi, rivers of phosphorescent algae. An ageless polis with one immortal tenant. He had thought he had found a kind of lonely peace there, until he heard the snakes for the first time. They had come for him, living flames of entropy flickering up from the molten iron core of the earth, looking for the rest-state. Lost in the center of his mineral whirlwind he had summoned them out of chaos. He violated the second law, the Law of Entropy, he was a reproach to the balance of existence. The servants of destruction undid everything he had worked on. Every tunnel, shaft, trench, revetement: back filled, demolished, undone. They nearly got him for good near Orlando, almost catching him in a living tomb. Panicked, he retreated to the surface.

He had gone down in 1791. He came back up in 1957, and was deafened, blinded, dumbfounded. He was blind already of course, his "eyes" just faceted crystals rattling around in a sapphire skull but his body was filled with magnetites, geodes, crystals. He could receive any signal, he couldn't stop receiving and during his silent exile the world had become filled with an invisible maelstrom of sounds and visions. He thought he would go mad, until she appeared on her first television appearance, the infamous and endearing interview. He saw her with his entire body. She was broadcast straight to his cold, hematite heart, she saturated him, her frequencies howling through his chained molecules. But he knew from the radio, the gossip columnists, the constant chatter of celebrity observers, that he was too late. She loved another: the sky boy.

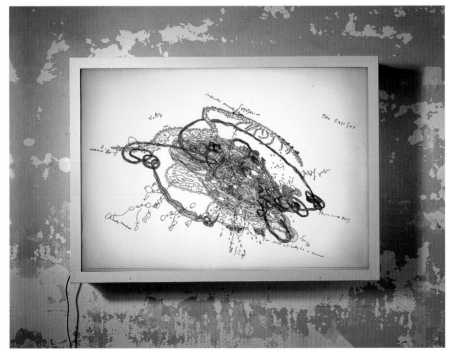

THE FAST SET

TOP AND BOTTOM RIGHT: INSTALLATION VIEWS: *THE FAST SET*, MUSEUM OF CONTEMPORARY ART, NORTH MIAMI, 2000

BOTTOM LEFT: *THE FAST SET* IN THE INSTALLATION *STACKED*, IN *UNNATURAL SCIENCE*, MASS MOCA, NORTH ADAMS, MASSACHUSETTS, 2000

CHAPEL PERILOUS   INSTALLATION VIEW OF *CHAPEL PERILOUS* IN "FAITH," ALDRICH MUSEUM OF CONTEMPORARY ART, RIDGEFIELD, CONNECTICUT, 2000

THE WORKING GROUP   INSTALLATION VIEW OF *THE WORKING GROUP* AT C/O ATLE GERHARDSEN, OSLO, NORWAY 1999

Matthew Ritchie

The Gamblers

Matthew Ritchie

Since it is almost impossible to understand them as they were then—as infinite points, bound in an indecomposable continuum—let's look at them as they would become….

On your left, the thin girl with the ashy skin and the shaved head with the dragon tattoo is Astoreth, "Asta" for short. She smiles awkwardly and ducks her head as you are introduced. She works in the Theoretical Physics department at MIT and in her spare time she cultivates an interest in LaPlace's probability studies and a drug habit. She was born a hermaphrodite and she plays Tarot poker. Next to her, the fat guy in the yellow shorts with a nasty sore on his leg covered in some kind of whitish salve is Bubba, he doesn't get up and he doesn't stop eating, he will later claim to be from Guam. Fine. He's a cryptologist—a code breaker, a numbers man. The key itself, the long golden-wanded decryption key, was all he brought to the table. The Asian woman artfully disguising the truth about her age, (somewhere in her late forties you would accurately guess), is Lilith. Fine grooves of command are etched in to her greenish complexion. She's the game manager, with a long time pachinko habit. Abaddon says a word that you think is "Haeccity" as you shake hands. He's a short, squarish man and beads of sweat and Hawking radiation are already forming on his shaved ebony head. He's a minister in the Union Vegetal in São Paulo and an expert in security systems and fencing stolen goods. He's wearing some kind of patterned smock over leather pants. He and Bubba know each other from way back, you can already tell they are not friends. He plays straight faro. Stanley himself is an attorney in a double breasted wool suit. He's solidly built, with a square cut graying beard and a prison pallor. His cellmates nicknamed him "Satan-El" when he argued a jailhouse brief that got him and two of the Satan's Slaves' motorcycle gang out with a retrial after serving two years of a five year hitch at Holmesburg Penitentiary, PA. While he was doing time he was a lab rat in the '72 Kligman LSD trials. He lost an eye in there and maybe that's why he plays roulette. One eye on the ball is all you need.

And finally, Lucky. It has been written that Lucifer was beautiful. Too perfect to look at without your eyes burning right out of your head, too desirable not to want to go blind. Just not true. There was always something missing from his bony good looks, humanity maybe. He was his usual crisp self as the evening began, his shirt starched to the razor edge of logic. Lucky played the markets: derivatives, commodities and human flesh….

…Asta was using a 97-card Florentine minchiate deck in a modified Royal spread. As she played she was scanning each card into a random number generator in her new G3 and then attaching them to a long piece of red wire from the tomb of Rachel. The wire was wound around the southwestern table leg, helping to lash a wand from the Adeptus Major rite of the Golden Dawn to the leg and simultaneously grounding her T1 line. She had already put the X on a hastily improvised game of "go" made of peanuts, played out earlier on the eastern edge of the table. Bubba had made a small mound of bananas, bread and canned corn, mashed them together and anointed them with spit and some old fluff from his pockets. He was slowly pushing lumps of the mess into a roughly heptagonal design in the northeastern corner while he scrawled random numbers on the inside of his shoe: "personal magic" he called it. He put the idiot back into idiot-savant. Lilith and Abaddon were working the Ouija board with a set of 64-letter alphabet tiles and using the results to place Superfecta bets on the races over in Cape Town. Stanley was a zombie player, sitting tight in the southeastern corner with his one blind eye turned inward. He was holding a leadpipe cinch in his left hand and rolling dice on the CP Mirror on off-number and one-roll bets with the other. Lucky was working the fax line and the NASDAQ ticker scanning for charmed derivatives and IPO's. Corporate voodoo, riding the northwestern web of Matlakali with a 4-D knucklebone program. He'd just placed a psychic bid on a biotech company operating out of Dublin. Despite all this effort, nothing was happening. They were on a cold streak and the house had the percentage.

THE GAMBLERS   INSTALLATION VIEW, *THE GAMBLERS*, BASILICO FINE ARTS, NEW YORK, 1998

Matthew Ritchie

The Hard Way

Matthew Ritchie

H°a rd° W°a y°

GALERIE METEO
BASILICO FINE ARTS
C/O · ATLE GERHARDSEN

They were seven, magnificently enough. Under cover of the unbearable light of the unending war, they made their way to the ladder of worlds.

AZAZEL

He loved everything and everyone. He wanted to seduce you, to explore you, to conquer you. He was greedy, uninhibited; he had a tongue that was two feet long. He started the whole thing, he was the first one to have sex with the early humans, the Neanderthals, he was the real troublemaker. He was a born politician, he had a high emotional IQ. He had a way with the ladies and a way with the men. He would fuck your pets and eat your furniture and then do it the other way around. He was your first lover and your last, he was every good time you ever had and every hangover all at once. He was bright red, covered in soft velvety fur, had poor posture and smelt strongly when wet. He was a party animal.

KASHDEJAH

She never took no for an answer. She was a strict carnivore, with more than a passing interest in the parts of the beast that other people overlooked. She avoided milk products. She could feel the child moving inside her; passing through the animal kingdoms as it grew and changed, from protozoa to fish; from fish to bird. She was stronger than the rest, an advocate of the Confucian system of justice—she would serve as judge, jury and executioner. She would rather die than bend, rather kill than break. She was a fanatic; every revolution needs one.

SHEMJAZA

He was sorry it had to be this way. Sorry about the lies, sorry about his own inevitable and disgraceful treachery. He was weak, although he could endure any pain. He knew they were wrong and he knew they were right. He was the loudest, the most enthusiastic; a leader. Nothing was radical enough for him, no declaration too grandiose. He would worry about the consequences later. His skin would be their banner, his eyes their gemstones, his body their temple. He was born under the sign of the Hanged Man and his skin gleamed in the tarnished light like newly washed gold. The land was dry but he would

water it with his tears. He knew he would pay for his lies. He knew it would hurt, a lot and he was sorry about that too.

KOKOBEL

It was like a talking to a memory. Burning leaves on an autumn day, a sense of time passing, the veins in your wrists becoming more obvious with age. No one was ever really clear if it even understood. It was Tamaii who talked to it, interpreted all that hooting and grinding; "Music of the Spheres" indeed. Of all of them, it had the least to lose and the least to gain. So many eyes; it seemed like thousands of them. Perhaps on its long voyages in the reaches, it had seen so much, so many strange and different things, that all change had come to seem relative. Whatever. It liked to travel.

MULCIBER

Mulciber was the builder. Spare and stony, the plates of its jade armor were weathered and pockmarked by the hard rains of radiation and the fires of the burning forests. No one was sure if there was even anything inside the armor anymore. Some people claimed you could see day-light shining right through it from certain angles. It spoke softly, as if it was whispering right into your ear. It had two thumbs on each hand. Its experiences with engineering had lent it a certain skepticism about the nature of the universe that led it to believe this would all end badly.

THE HARD WAY

TOP LEFT AND RIGHT: INSTALLATION VIEWS, *THE HARD WAY, CHAPTER II*, BASILICO FINE ARTS, NEW YORK, 1996

BOTTOM LEFT: INSTALLATION VIEW, *THE HARD WAY, CHAPTER I*, GALERIE MÉTÉO, PARIS, 1996

BOTTOM RIGHT: INSTALLATION VIEW, *THE HARD WAY, CHAPTER III*, C/O ATLE GERHARDSEN, OSLO, NORWAY, 1996

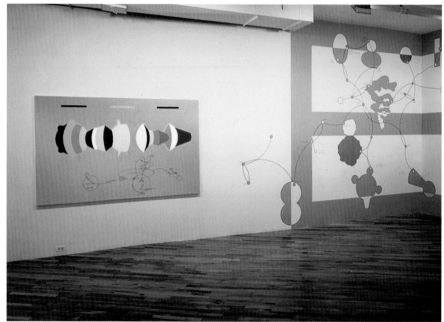

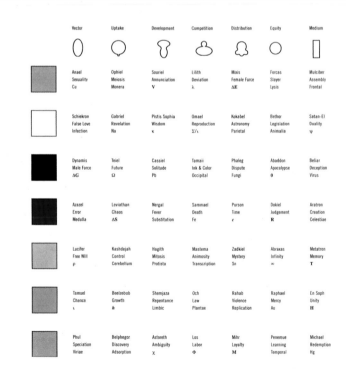

WORKING MODEL

TOP LEFT AND RIGHT: INSTALLATION VIEWS OF *WORKING MODEL*, BASILICO FINE ARTS, NEW YORK, 1995

BOTTOM LEFT: INSTALLAION VIEW OF *THE GOD GAME*, 1995, IN *WORKING MODEL*, BASILICO FINE ARTS, NEW YORK, 1995

BOTTOM RIGHT: *WORKING MODEL* (DETAIL), 1995. INK ON PAPER. 20 x 18 INCHES (51 x 46 CM). COLLECTION THE ARTIST

	Vector	Uptake	Development	Competition	Distribution	Equity	Medium
	Anael / Sexuality / Cu	Ophiel / Meiosis / Monera	Souriel / Annunciation / V	Lilith / Deviation / λ	Mixis / Female Force / ΔE	Forcas / Slayer / Lysis	Mulciber / Assembly / Frontal
	Schiekron / False Love / Infection	Gabriel / Revelation / Na	Pistis Sophia / Wisdom / κ	Omael / Reproduction / Σ/ι	Kokabel / Astronomy / Parietal	Bethor / Legislation / Animalia	Satan-El / Duality / ψ
	Dynamis / Male Force / ΔG	Teiel / Future / Ω	Cassiel / Solitude / Pb	Tamaii / Ink & Color / Occipital	Phaleg / Dispute / Fungi	Abaddon / Apocalypse / θ	Beliar / Deception / Virus
	Azazel / Error / Medulla	Leviathan / Chaos / ΔS	Nergal / Fever / Substitution	Sammael / Death / Fe	Purson / Time / c	Dokiel / Judgement / R	Aratron / Creation / Celestiae
	Lucifer / Free Will / ρ	Kashdejah / Control / Cerebellum	Hagith / Mitosis / Protista	Mastema / Animosity / Transcription	Zadkiel / Mystery / Sn	Abraxas / Infinity / ∞	Metatron / Memory / T
	Tamuel / Chance / ι	Beelzebub / Growth / ħ	Shemjaza / Repentance / Limbic	Och / Law / Plantae	Rahab / Violence / Replication	Raphael / Mercy / Au	En Soph / Unity / H
	Phul / Speciation / Viriae	Belphegor / Discovery / Adsorption	Astoreth / Ambiguity / χ	Los / Labor / Φ	Mihr / Loyalty / M	Penemue / Learning / Temporal	Michael / Redemption / Hg

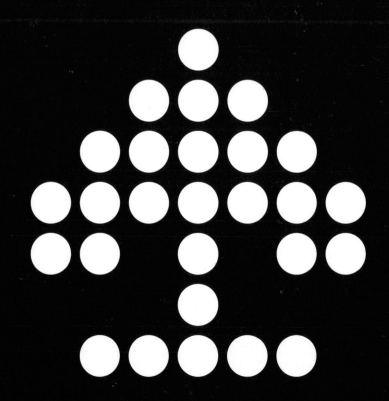

Sources: Selected Readings

From P.C.W. Davies, "Why is the Physical World so Comprehensible?" in *Complexity, Entropy, and the Physics of Information*, SFI Studies in the Sciences of Complexity, Vol. VIII, Ed. W.H. Zurek, Addison-Wesley, 1990.

Why is the Physical World so Comprehensible?

A vexing scientific mystery of longstanding concerns the peculiar conjunction of simplicity and complexity that pervades the universe. We believe that the underlying laws of physics are simple in form, yet the actual states of the world are highly complex. It is only in recent years that any sort of general understanding of the source of this complexity has emerged.

The most striking feature of many complex systems is their non-random nature. The universe is populated by distinct classes of recognizable things: galaxies, stars, crystals, clouds, bacteria, people. Given the limitless variety of ways in which matter and energy can arrange themselves, almost all of which would be "random," the fact that the physical world is a coherent collection of mutually tolerant, quasi-stable entities is surely a key scientific fact in need of explanation.

The non-random nature of cosmic complexity is captured by the concept of organization, or, to use a more fashionable word, depth. According to the best cosmological theories, the universe began in an exceedingly simple state. Indeed, the initial state might well have been essentially smooth empty space. It is hard to think of anything more "shallow." All the depth that has arisen in the universe is the result of a sequence of self-organizing and self-complexifying processes that have occurred since the initial bang. The epithet "creation" in connection with the big bang seems a serious misnomer, since almost all the creative activity that has generated the richness and variety of the present state occurred after the big bang.

The seemingly unidirectional advance of complex organization, or depth, imposes on the universe an arrow of time, which is related to, but distinct from, that due to the second law of thermodynamics. Some people have perceived an element of paradox in the growth of organization in a universe in which entropy always rises. True, the former arrow does challenge the spirit of the second law, which predicts continual degeneration. But there is no conflict with the letter of the law. Self-organization costs entropy. But whereas entropy is a measure of information loss, organization (or depth) refers instead to the quality of information. Entropy and depth are not each other's negatives.

Among the more interesting complex organized systems to have arisen thus is the human brain. Containing as it does an internal representation of the physical world, the brain stands in an unusual relationship with the world. And here the conjunction of simplicity and complexity is inverted: the brain is incredibly complex, but the mental states that it supports make the world seem deceptively simple. We are able to function as human beings because our mental model of the world bestows upon it a coherent unity. When we talk about "understanding" some aspect of nature, we mean slotting the phenomena associated therewith into our existing mental model of "how things are out there."

Is this process of understanding a surprise? Does it tell us anything significant about the structure of the brain, or the world, or both? Many people have puzzled about such issues. Why is the universe knowable? After all, given the enormous complexity and interconnectedness of the physical world, how can we know anything without knowing everything? Indeed, how can we know anything at all?

As a starting point in addressing these tough questions, let us agree at least on the following statements:

• There exists a real external world which contains certain regularities. These regularities can be understood, at least in part, by a process of rational enquiry called the scientific method.

• Science is not merely a game or charade. Its results capture, however imperfectly, some aspect of reality. Thus these regularities are real properties of the physical universe and not just human inventions or delusions.

In making these assumptions one has to eschew extreme idealistic philosophies, such as those in which the mind somehow imposes the regularities on the world in order to make sense of it. Unless one accepts that the regularities are in some sense objectively real, one might as well stop doing science.

As science progresses, so some regularities become systematized as laws, or deductions from them. At this epoch the laws found in our textbooks image only imperfectly the actual regularities. Two points of view can be detected among practicing scientists regarding the ontological status of these laws. The first is that there exist "real" laws, or "the correct set" of laws, to which our current theories are only an approximation. As science progresses so we converge upon the "true" laws of the universe, which are regarded as eternal, timeless, and transcendent of the physical states.

By contrast, some scientists deny that there are any "true" laws "out there," existing independently of scientific enquiry. What we call laws, they maintain, are simply our attempts to cope with the world by ordering our experiences in a systematic way. The only laws are our laws, and they are to be judged solely on utilitarian grounds, i.e., they are neither true nor false, but merely more or less useful to us. My impression is that many scientists who practice what one might loosely call applied science incline to the latter philosophy, while those engaged in "fundamental" research, for example, on quantum cosmology or the unification program, adopt the former position.

The issue of whether the laws of nature are discovered or invented is sidestepped if we view the world algorithmically. The existence of regularities may be expressed by saying that the world is algorithmically compressible. Given some data set, the job of the scientist is to find a suitable compression, which expresses the causal linkages involved. For example, the positions of the planets in the solar system over some interval constitute a compressible data set, because Newton's laws may be used to link these positions at all times to the positions (and velocities) at some initial time. In this case, Newton's laws supply the necessary algorithm to achieve the compression.

Viewed this way, the question "Why is the universe knowable?" reduces to "Why is the universe algorithmically compressible?" and "Why are human beings so adept at discovering the compressions?"

From *Laws of the Game* by Manfred M. Eigen and Ruthild Winkler, copyright Translation Copyright (c) 1981 by Alfred A. Knopf Inc. Used by permission of Alfred A. Knopf, a division of Random House.

Laws of the Game: How the Principles of Nature Govern Chance

CREATION OR REVELATION? In his lectures, the Göttingen physicist Robert Wichard Pohl often concluded his elucidation of a point by saying: "And that gives us all the more cause for wonder." By this he did not mean that the success of an experiment just conducted was a cause for wonder, although such success might well have appeared miraculous considering what simple means he used to demonstrate the most complex phenomena. The important point is that he made this statement after everything was explained and we might have thought there was nothing left to wonder about.

Wonder is, of course, the source of all inquiry. We begin by standing astonished and helpless in the face of the incomprehensible. Curiosity and a thirst for knowledge grow, the deeper we penetrate into the mysterious darkness and the more facts we illuminate. Once we have gathered these facts, we begin to sort them, compare them, and correlate them until we are able to grasp the overall context in which they belong. But does the solution of a problem necessarily put an end to our wonder? Will the miraculous eventually be researched out of our lives?

In his book *The Pleasure Areas*,[55] the English neurophysiologist Herbert James Campbell describes all the knowledge we have gained in recent years about the localization of pain and pleasure in the central nervous system of higher organisms and about the role they play in directing behavior. Some passages in this book suggest that expanding knowledge is putting an end to wonder. But the exciting results of neurophysiological research in this area by no means indicate that the miraculous will cease to exist if we come to understand it. The understanding of phenomena still does not answer Leibniz's question "Why is there something instead of nothing?"

The central theme of this chapter has been the miraculous order of living things, order not so much in the sense of order in space and time—although life does appear in spatial form and in temporal rhythms—as in the sense of organization, information and uniqueness. Every single protein molecule is unique. It was selected from a vastly complex variety of alternative structures and combinations in which the same building blocks are "systematically" arranged in a different order and sequence. If we had one example each of all possible protein structures, we would have so many that

they would not fit into the entire universe even if they were jammed in as tightly as possible. The fraction of protein structures that have occurred in the entire history of the earth is so minute that the existence of efficient enzyme molecules borders on the miraculous.

Human beings are quick to categorize the miraculous. They attach an adjective to it and assign it a place in their world-view:

incomprehensible — God — religion
deterministic — matter — dialectic
accidental — nothing — existentialism

These combinations are by no means fixed. The terms can be grouped together differently:

God and natural law: "I believe in Spinoza's god, who is manifest in the harmony of all being, not in a god that is preoccupied with the fate and actions of men." This was Albert Einstein's answer to a telegram from the New York rabbi H.S. Goldstein, asking "Do you believe in God?"

Nothing and dialectic: "We agree that there is no human nature. In other words, every epoch develops according to dialectic laws, and men are determined by their times, not by human nature." Jean-Paul Sartre made this remark in a discussion of his essay *Existentialism Is a Humanism*.[56]

Jacques Monod rejects—and in our opinion rightly so—any of the anthropocentric explanations for the phenomenon of life that are common to most philosophies and religions. In animism, which he defines as "the consciousness that human beings derive from the strongly teleological workings of their own central nervous systems and that they project into the natural world," Monod sees a violation of all objective knowledge.

However, the step from an invocation of absolute and blind chance[52] ("Pure chance, nothing but chance, absolute, blind freedom as the foundation of the miraculous structure of evolution…") to an a priori rejection of any attempt "to prove, on the basis of thermodynamic calculations, that chance alone cannot explain selection in the process of evolution,"[57] is not a large one. Such an attempt, if successful, would negate Monod's intention to derive the necessity "for an existential attitude toward life and

society…from objective scientific knowledge." But is this judgment of Monod's not a new attempt to derive a human-oriented theory of being from the behavior of matter? Would this not be, in other words, a new animism? Otto Friedrich Bollnow characterized this theory in relation to human beings as follows:[58]

If we try to summarize the anthropological principle of existential philosophy in a few words, we could say that in men there is an ultimate inner core designated, by a term characteristic of this philosophy, as existence, which has by nature no permanent manifestation because it only realizes itself in the moment and, in the next moment, ceases to exist in that form. On the existential level, this philosophy claims, there is no permanence in life processes and therefore no preserving beyond the moment what has been achieved, much less any constant progress. There is only an individual leap upward, which grows out of the gathered forces of the moment. It is followed by a plunge downward into the state of drab, uneventful life, which may, at some later moment, give rise to another leap upward.

Notes:

52. Monod, Jacques, *Chance and Necessity*. New York: Alfred A. Knopf, 1972.

55. Campbell, H.J., *The Pleasure Areas: A New Theory of Behavior*. New York: Delacorte Press, 1973.

56. Sartre, Jean Paul, *Drei Essays* (Three Essays). Frankfurt am Main/Berlin/Vienna: Verlag Ulstein, 1973.

57. Monod, Jacques, "L'evolution microscopique (Microscopic Evolution)," report on a lecture, *Neue Zürcher Zeitung*, February 19, 1975.

58. Bollnow, O.F., *Existenzphilosophie und Pädagogik* (Existential Philosophy and Pedagogy), Stuttgart: W. Kohlhammer Verlag, 1959.

From Christopher J. Isham and Konstantina Savvidou, "Time and Modern Physics," in *Time*, ed. Katinka Ridderbos (London: Cambridge University Press, 2002). Reprinted with the permission of Cambridge University Press.

Time and Modern Physics

Time is a child playing gambling;
For the kingdom is for the simple.

—Heraclitus

THE SUBJECT OF TIME

The subject of 'time' exercises a universal fascination. In no small part this is due to the genuinely interdisciplinary nature of the issues that arise. Thus questions about the nature of time occur in areas as disparate as physics, biology, psychology, philosophy, poetry (think of the work of T.S. Elliot), visual art, theology, music (for example, in the chanting of plainsong) and many more.

Some of these topics are covered in other chapters in this book, but in all cases—or, at least, in the more academic disciplines—a basic question is how the concept of time fits into the underlying metaphysical structure of the subject concerned. Thus, for us, a key issue is the role played by time in the foundations of modern physics. And, as theoretical physicists, we are particularly concerned with how the answer to this question relates to the various mathematical structures that are involved in the physicist's account of time.

Let us begin by remarking that there are two quite different ways in which time has been viewed by physical scientists: these are known as the absolute and relational ideas of time. In essence, the difference comes down to whether or not we grant time (and space) an existence independent of material objects and processes. According to the absolute view of time (and space), time (and space) simply form the 'arena' of physics; the background structure within whose framework all of physics is necessarily phrased. On this view, material processes take place against the background of an independent 'something' called time (and space). Newtonian physics and the theory of special relativity are good examples of theoretical frameworks of this type.

On the other hand, the relational view denies time (and space) an existence independent of material objects and processes. On this view, time exists only by virtue of the existence of matter and material events. Thus the concept of time is dependent in some way on the idea of matter. This view is famously associated with the names Leibniz and Mach. General relativity is arguably a theory of this type, although in its typical applications it also assumes certain absolute structures.

To a significant extent, modern physics oscillates uneasily between these two perspectives on time. One important issue is the way in which they are related. For example, what is the role of a 'clock' in this respect? Let us consider a wristwatch. On the one hand, it is made of matter and in that sense its temporal qualities are naturally associated with the second view. On the other hand, when we talk of a 'good' watch, we typically mean the extent to which it measures accurately the background absolute time of Newtonian physics—a concept that clearly accords with the first view of space and time.

But what about an atomic clock, which also is made of (quantum) matter? In this case we typically talk about the clock defining time, rather than measuring it. But what then is meant by a 'good' atomic clock: are some definitions of time 'better' than others, and how are they related to each other, and to the background time of Newtonian physics?

Clearly, one format for a chapter on 'Time and Modern Physics' would be to survey the different ideas of time in the classical and quantum versions of Newtonian physics, special relativity and general relativity. However, we have elected to follow a different route and to concentrate instead on two particular ways in which time arises in modern physics: as the parameter in temporal logic and as the parameter of dynamics. This will allow us to touch on many of the basic ideas concerning time, as well as to discuss some very recent ideas about time in physics.

TWO ROLES FOR TIME

The nature of time is something that much occupied St. Augustine; perhaps because, as he explains in his *Confessions*, he had such a 'good time' when he was a young man! Whatever the case may be, it is appropriate in our case to start with the following well-known excerpt from *The Confessions*:

What then is time? If no one asks me I know; if I want to explain it to a questioner; I do not know. But at any rate this much I dare affirm I know: that if nothing passed there would be no past time; if nothing were approaching, there would be no future time; if nothing were then there would be no present time.

The ideas implied here are as profound and relevant today as when the saint first stated them. One such is the universally acknowledged fact that 'time' is an elusive concept: in one sense we think we know exactly to what it refers, but when we try to pin it down it slips away—like a chimera, a will-o'-the-wisp. However, of more direct relevance to our present task is the several different roles for time that are implicit in Augustine's remarks. This theme is anticipated in the earlier comments of Aristotle, in his *Physics*, on the notion of time:

But when we perceive a distinct before and after, then we speak of time; for this is just what time is, the calculable measure or dimension of motion with respect to before-and-afterness. Time, then, is not movement, but that by which movement can be numerically estimated. And as motion is a continuous flux, so is time; but at any given moment time is the same everywhere, for the 'now' itself is identical in its essence, but the relations into which it enters differ in different connections, and it is the 'now' that marks off time as before and after. But this 'now' which is identical everywhere, itself retains its identity in one sense, but does not in another; for inasmuch as the point in the flux of time which it marks is changing the 'now' too differs perpetually, but inasmuch as at every moment it is performing its essential function of dividing the past and future, it retains its identity.

Copyright 1998 From "Vision and Cognition," by Krzysztof Pomian in *Picturing Science Producing Art*, ed. Caroline A. Jones and Peter Galison. Reproduced by permission of Routledge/Taylor & Francis Books, Inc.

Vision and Cognition

If the intellect could in addition directly grasp things themselves, it would be entitled to proceed to the critique of senses founded on its capacity of confronting their data with objects that are their causes. So it was according to Descartes. But Hume and Kant deny all intellectual intuition. The intellect is for them nothing more than the capacity to associate or synthesize sensations and thus to produce representations, ideas, or phenomena. These productions cannot however confront things themselves, because they remain irreparably isolated from them. Yet besides the senses and the intellect, we have no faculty of cognition, and thus we have no immediate relation with things themselves. Conclusion: the belief that we remain enclosed in the world of human representations is inevitable, insofar as we accept the indirect character of sensory cognition, deny the possibility of intellectual intuition, and refuse to admit any cognition that would be neither sensory nor intellectual, as if the division in these two categories was at the same time exhaustive and utterly disjunctive.

Yet this last assumption can no longer be accepted, if it was even acceptable in the times of Hume and Kant, to say nothing of later in the nineteenth century and into the twentieth. It can no longer be accepted not because of a discovery of some extrasensory metaphysical cognition; such an event never occurred. But we practice every day and at an enormous scale a kind of cognition that, despite its being extrasensory, is nevertheless a physical fact. I refer here obviously to the cognition through the agency of instruments of observation and measurement. I shall try now to sketch some characteristic features of this type of cognition, in order to show that the very fact we are practicing it obliges us to abandon the model of cognition as production.

Instruments of observation and measurement are not simple extensions of senses. Such an opinion could probably be accepted with regard to an optical microscope or a telescope, although already these instruments as far as they enable us to see objects beyond the reach of the naked eye, introduce a cognition qualitatively different from the only one the latter is able to practice; on this point Descartes as well as Kant would agree.[58] But even if one could reduce this difference to a simple widening of the visual field and an increase in the number of objects grasped by sight (without being aware of the fact that sight is transformed by such moves beyond what it was before Galileo), such an attempt would seem simply incongruous with regard to a Geiger counter, a spectrograph, a radio telescope, or a particle accelerator. In all these cases indeed the instruments we deal with function according to principles sharply different from those governing our sensory organs (although their data might take visual or auditory forms). Such instruments enable us to apply cognition to objects that would otherwise be inaccessible through differences in their very manner of being from ordinary objects of our macroscopic world. To characterize such instruments of observation and measurement as extensions of our senses is to erase without any justification the essential difference between two types of cognition.

This does not mean that instruments belong to the sphere of intellectual cognition. For they are not simple materializations of theories. It is true that without theory one could not build them or discuss their results, i.e., establish in what limits their indications express their effective interactions with objects they are applied to. There is however a deep difference between the statement according to which a theory is necessary in order to build and to use instruments and the statement according to which either may be reduced to a theory. The first is obviously true. The second either means that instruments do not bring anything unforeseen by the theory from which they proceed, or it has no definite meaning. It is therefore either manifestly false or obscure. And it is manifestly false because there are countless examples of results of observations and of experiments no theories have foreseen, without even mentioning those that contradicted theories that were apparently very well grounded.

This cognition through the agency of instruments of observation and measurement is therefore an extrasensory but nonetheless physical cognition. And extra-intellectual—but also productive of elements of discourse: of images, of indications displayed on screens, of photographs, of different types of recordings, and so forth. It is a cognition sui generis. And its particularly striking character is its being an indirect cognition: what we receive as a result of an observation or an experiment is either the image of an interaction between an instrument and the object to which it is applied, or a set of parameters that describe such an interaction. This enables us, thanks to our knowledge of the instrument used, to infer the properties of the object itself, holding off on the theory, within the limits established by laws of physics. The possibility of reproducing an observation or an experiment and of controlling one instrument through its confrontation with others of the same kind gives us good reason to think that we deal indeed with natural objects, and not with artifacts.

In contradistinction to sensory cognition, which seems immutable (although it has its history too), instrumental cognition evolves in a spectacular manner through an enrichment of the panoply of instruments and their improvement. By its very nature, it creates a history. As this history proceeds, objects on which we are informed by instruments become more and more distant, from us: distant in space, distant in time, distant because of their dimensions, distant, in the end, because of their strangeness with respect to laws of the macroscopic world in which we live. In order to be able to have a correct representation of these objects and in order to be able to think about them, it was necessary to modify even some of the most unquestionable of our assumptions concerning, in particular, the ideas of space and of time, the ideas of identity, the idea of determinism, and so forth.

The history of physics for approximately a century shows clearly, through paradoxes, contradictions, and difficulties (all of which provoke controversies), the incapacity of the usual language and of the stock of images derived from everyday experience to master conceptually the new universe progressively unveiled. It shows also a struggle with the usual language and with intellectual habits rooted in everyday experience, which, in the end, were both completely overthrown. It shows, in a word, that physicists had constantly to learn anew how to imagine and how to think in order to adapt themselves to results furnished by instruments, and to derive from them conclusions able to be translated in the language that may be understood by instruments and thus to be submitted to a test of observation or experiment....

Notes:
58. See Joel Snyder's comments on this issue in the present volume and his discussion of Ian Hacking's position.

From Arthur S. McGrade, *The Political Thought of William of Ockham* (London: Cambridge University Press, 1974). Reprinted with the permission of Cambridge University Press.

The Political Thought of William of Ockham

INDIVIDUALS

Ockham sought to reduce collisions between the major institutions of his time by narrowing the essential functions of secular government on the one hand and emphasizing the specifically spiritual character of ecclesiastical government on the other. In theory at least, this also liberated much of human life from immediate institutional control of any kind. Such a result was no accident. Whether in appealing to gospel liberty or to Aristotle's unfavorable assessment of despotism, Ockham accorded great value to personal freedom. This was not merely an inner freedom to be found in subordination to higher principles and authorities but the power of individuals—free subjects,[7] who existed for themselves and not for the sake of their rulers—to be masters of their own actions, to enjoy the rights and liberties conceded to all mortals by God and nature. In this respect, Ockham's political works, especially when read in conjunction with his earlier ethical writings, are an important contribution to Western thought about human rights and the dignity of individuals. By the same token, however, although his moderate doctrine of secular government and his emphasis on inner psychological processes have clear affinities with the ideas of Augustine, Ockham's work signals the end of political Augustinism[8] and the hierocratically inspired descending thesis of government with its resulting program of moulding society from above. Does this mean a rejection, in effect if not in so many words, of classical and medieval ideals of communal wholeness, unity, and order? In Ockham's thought these ideals no longer function as principles justifying a unitary political system, but we should not conclude too hastily that they have no effective status in a world of individuals....

KNOWLEDGE AND POLITICAL POWER

...There is another side to Ockham's difference with tradition on the relation between knowledge and action. It concerns the importance of understanding being possessed by subjects as well as rulers. Ockham held that human and Christian freedom consisted of self-direction rather than unreflective participation in a broader social whole. If this is the case, it becomes essential that free individuals understand for themselves the legal, moral,

and religious truths on which they ought to act. Among other things, the subject of any government ought to know in a relatively precise way the character and extent of his ruler's legitimate power over him, and the individual believer is entitled to an understanding of the Christian faith. Because the knowledge required for human life should be shared by all, it follows that those who possess such knowledge must explain it to others, not merely provide authoritative pronouncements. At the same time, because Ockham thought there was a science of morals and objective knowledge of at least some of God's intentions as revealed in Scripture, the man who has knowledge and can explain it, whether he be a prelate or an academic expert, is compelled to bring this knowledge to bear for the attainment of good ends. He cannot be the morally neutral servant of institutions which themselves determine the ends of action in arbitrary ways. Ockham was led to these conclusions partly by his own speculative principles but most immediately by the necessity he felt for dealing with the problem of papal heresy. Accordingly, his clearest account of the relations between knowledge and power is given in *I Dialogus*, a work which has impressed many readers as an attack on the foundations of medieval Christian society. It may be well to consider, however, that Ockham's defense of autonomy and self-consciousness, in spite of its modernity and potentially disruptive quality, was a genuine development of classical and medieval principles. In happier circumstances, this development might have been compatible with other traditions in practice as well as in theory.

OCKHAM AS A CONSTRUCTIVE POLITICAL THINKER

The preceding review suggests that Ockham's approach to politics was in more than one sense constructive. The basic principles on which he worked were positive rather than skeptical. They were either principles already professed by his society or, as in the case of Aristotle's analysis of royal and tyrannical government, morally positive philosophical ideas. His sharpest personal attacks were delivered on behalf of Christian orthodoxy, and his demand for institutional justice was also an attack on what he perceived as disturbances of the traditional order. Far from being a political skeptic, Ockham was so insistent on handling practical problems

in a principled way and so critical of arbitrary, merely authoritarian, exercises of power that the reader may be inclined to criticize him for intolerance. He was outraged at what he took to be the irrationality of the world around him, especially of the Avignonese papacy, but rejected the cynical view that truth, justice, and sincere piety must generally be sacrificed to obtain spiritual and temporal tranquility. Ockham demanded tranquility and virtue as well. In this he was perhaps narrow, visionary, or naïve but certainly not a skeptic.

Ockham's political work was not merely an emphatic assertion of principle, however. It was constructive in the further sense of being an attempt to promote stable and effective institutional structures. To be sure, the whole point of institutions in Ockham's view was to provide for the exercise of legitimate individual rights and freedoms, but, as we have seen, he not only denied in the abstract that life without government was possible in this world but discussed the problems of government in detail and with attention to traditional legal sources and techniques. The much debated question of his influence in the conciliar era should be approached with this aspect of his work in mind. Almost in the nature of the case, the educated and influential men who were able to put his ideas into practice in the fourteenth and fifteenth centuries were respectable ecclesiastics who would have viewed his personal history with grave misgivings.

Notes:

7. Ockham speaks always of subjects rather than citizens, perhaps because he did not wish to disguise the relationship of superior and inferior obtaining between those who have power and those who do not. The idea of citizenship also loses some of its relevance in his thought because of his comparatively negative and instrumental view of government. The full-fledged member of an Aristotelian *polis* is naturally called a citizen because he achieves so much of his own fulfillment in and through the community he participates in organizing.

8. On political Augustinism and the problem of its relation to Augustine's own thought, see H.-X. Arquillière, *L'augustinisme politique*, 2nd ed. (Paris, 1955).

From *Science, Action, and Fundamental Theology* by Helmut Peukert. English translation © 1984 by The Massachusetts Institute of Technology. This work originally appeared in German as *Wissenschaftstheorie–Handlungstheorie–Fundamentale Theologie: Analysen zu Ansatz und Status theologischer Theoriebildung,* © 1976 by Patmos-Verlag, Düsseldorf, Federal Republic of Germany.

Science, Action & Fundamental Theology

A TYPOLOGY OF ATTEMPTS TO DEVELOP A METATHEORY OF THEOLOGY

The basic ideas underlying the history of the modern sciences claim universal status because they rest on the principle of critique. The theory of these sciences therefore claims to develop the criteria for the meaning of all theoretical statements. As a matter of fact, a theory of science emerges with the claim to delineate metatheoretically the framework for theology.

The concern of this section is to investigate specific fundamental possibilities for such attempts to establish a metatheory of theology. As distinct from the previous section, we are not here testing fully developed conceptions, but rather basically possible positions, even if this investigation itself takes its starting point from specific proposals of its own. The function of this section is to exclude insufficient strategies for the solution to these problems by pointing out their inner aporias and so to outline in some detail the solution sought by saying what it is not.

THE CONCEPTION OF THEOLOGY ON THE TRADITIONAL MODEL OF AN EMPIRICAL-ANALYTICAL SCIENCE

The convincing claim of scientific critique led to the fact that its standard did not remain external to theology itself but, by way of historical-critical inquiry, has even carried the day in theology itself. Modern theology is unthinkable without this solidarity in critique.

However, the question arises whether or not theology as a whole can be conceived on the model of an empirical-critical science as understood by the theory of science in recent decades. It should be clear that everything depends on how one assesses the results of the discussion of the problem of foundations.

This question may be exemplarily explicated in the problem area of a theory of religious speech. The basic problem of any such theory is to indicate precisely what relation to reality religious discourse has and what criteria satisfy its claims to truth. This dovetails into many individual subquestions: Does religious speech have its own semantics, distinct from other modes of speech? If so, in what ways can it be distinguished, and how can this special semantics be formulated? Can religious discourse be differentiated and identified syntactically? Do images, metaphors, and models in religious speech have their own independent function? Is it sufficient merely to investigate particular concepts within religious discourse, or must their meaning be discerned from situationally related texts? Besides a universal pragmatics, is there something like a special pragmatics of religious speech acts and speech situations? All these questions could be asked within a traditional theory of language. If theology is to be understood as a theory of religious discourse, then this raises the question of whether theology merely coincides with this theory of language.

Decisive questions remain, however. If what is characteristic of scientific theory formation is the objectivation of a realm of objects, then the inquirer as subject (or, rather, the community of inquirers) is missing; it emerges only in limit problems, such as those points in inquiry where decisions have to be made about the metatheoretical suppositions of a theory or an entire research program. The place of the subject in these limit problems can be seen to emerge in the development from Wittgenstein to Kuhn and Feyerabend.

What stands out as the characteristic feature of religious discourse, as opposed to scientific theory formation, is that the subjects, or more precisely the parties engaged in speech, are constitutive for the realm of objects of religious discourse. A theory of religious discourse, then, faces the question whether it can be developed as an objectivating construction about speaking subjects, or whether in its basic structure it must have the character of self-reflection, which seeks to clarify one's own actions.

We have seen that such questions are characteristic for the problematic of the foundations of the social sciences. The basic problem that arose there was whether theories about subjects do not at the same time always have to represent enlightening, ideological-critical self-reflection. It need not yet be decided here how theology is to be conceived within such a framework. What now must be debated is whether theology can be thought of in terms of the model of objectivating theoretical constructions. There is obviously something self-contradictory about affirming such a claim. An objectivating theory of subjects would have to exclude theory-forming subjects, along with their metatheoretical decisions, from its theory; however, the very principle of critique would necessarily stand in the way of an uncritical acceptance of such a model.

In an objectivating conception, one regresses behind the state of the problem fought for in the theological discussions of the last two centuries, primarily in theological hermeneutics. Even in theology, regression in not a possible problem-solving behavior. All attempts in which theology simply assumes the principles of "Critical Rationalism" fall under this criticism, especially since such a view does not even do justice to the present state of the theory of science.[25] Theology also may not simply retreat to the stage of an objectivistic scholasticism that does not even understand its own foundations. Similarly, attempts to transform an objectivistically understood linguistics into a metatheory for theology would also have to be criticized. I shall discuss several such proposals later.

Assuming on the one hand that the discussion of foundations in the theory of science from Gödel and Tarski through Popper and Carnap to Kuhn and Feyerabend reaches dimensions traditionally ascribed to hermeneutics and, on the other hand, that hermeneutics can no longer be seen as the single "method" in the classical humanistic disciplines but rather that "understanding" is still possible only by integrating analytic procedures, the question is posed for theology even more stringently as to the status of a theory that, as an empirical theory, includes reflection on subjects and their performances.

Notes:

25. The consequences of accepting these standards can be seen in the work of Grabner-Haider. He tries to escape the obvious contradictions that result from accepting these standards by dividing theology into two realms, one that makes statements and another that does not. For the former, this sentence could be considered a basic metatheoretical axiom: "Everything that God has revealed and the Church teaches us to believe is true." (*Theorie der Theologie,* p. 130). After the acceptance of this "basic dogma," the axiomatization of religious language is hardly problematic. But this ignores the entire hermeneutic discussion in which theology labors concerning this "everything that." If one attempts to determine the propositional part of theology in a theory of speech acts conceived independent of it, then there result both the problems of speech-act theory discussed above and the ultimate fixation of this false dichotomy in theology.

From Milo Rigaud, *Secrets of Voodoo*, (San Francisco: City Lights Books, 1985).

Secrets of Voodoo

SYMBOLS OF VOODOO

Voodoo has many important symbols to aid its magic. Only through the use of these symbols is the Voodoo adherent able to attain the assistance of the loas in helping him with his earthly problems.

THE VÈVÈS

The *vèvès* are without any doubt the most spectacular ceremonial factor of Voodoo. The vèvès are designs traced upon the ground of the peristyle or the oum'phor, or upon all sorts of objects, even ritual food. In the region of Port-au-Prince the vèvès are made with great care so that they are clearly visible and almost geometrically flawless. Elsewhere, however, it is made carelessly and crudely; and in some regions it is not used at all, for example in the oum'phors in the neighborhood of Gonaives.

The vèvès represent *figures of the astral forces* in a different way than the asson does. Their manufacture in the oum'phor is the reproduction by Voodoo magic of the astral forces themselves. This fact signifies that the vèvès, considered as astral forces, are necessarily personified by the star-ancestors whose cult is voodoo—these ancestors being themselves personified by the loas, the spirits, the voudoun, or the mystères that "mount" the Voodooists.

In the course of Voodoo ceremonies, the reproduction of the astral forces represented by the vèvès obliges the loas (who are representations of heavenly bodies, stars, and planets) to descend to earth. On first consideration, this may appear improbable; however, nothing is truer, more obvious, or more palpable, and the explanation, given here for the first time, can be easily verified. As a visitor at a Voodoo service, one has only to consider the interrelation of the ritual factors as explained here in order to be easily convinced.

Depending upon the rite, the vèvè is traced with wheat flour, corn meal, Guinea-flour (wood ashes), powdered leaves, red brick powder, rice powder (face powder), and even gunpowder, powdered charcoal, bark, or roots.

As a rule, the milder rites such as the Rada, a solar rite, require white or yellow wheat. Tradition, though not always respected, demands that corn meal be used for the intermediate or less mild rites, whereas red brick powder or red dust or ashes belong to the fire rites whose cabalistic agents can, if need be, serve upon the *points-chauds* (hot points)—not that these rites are fundamentally or necessarily evil, but rather because they have a greater tendency to burn when they are improperly or imprudently employed.

The powder of leaves, if the leaves are of the soothing variety, can be used for the mystères of the *points-frettes* (cold-points). If the powder is made of noxious leaves or merely of the "stinging" variety, it can "walk with" the so-called "Bois-Piquant" (pungent wood) loas, the loas of the fiery rites: the *Pethro* and the *Zandor*.

Gunpowder serves to pecipitate magically the mystères.

Face powder, scarcely used in Haiti, if at all, for vèvès, is traditionally employed for the brilliant mystères that "walk on the resplendent points" of the Sun: *Erzulie Za-Gaza*, the mystère *Joltière Viscière*, and *Legba Brillant Soleil.* For face powder symbolizes the purification, at a very high degree, of the ceremonial and sacrificial material. These brilliant mystères correspond necessarily to the most splendid stellar and planetary elements in the whole Voodoo organization of Legba Ati-Bon, not only because the magic system of Legba *is* the solar system, but also because the formula which designates the various types of powder is a part of Legba's own name: *ati-n. Ati-n*, then, means *ati-* ("magic wood" or "magic master") and *-n* ("of astral space").

Therefore, in considering this vèvè which is a synthesis of space, of the astral, and of their powers through Legba, we see a synthesis of the vèvè principle.

In the ritual geometry of Voodoo, most of the vèvès include the serpent as a symbol of the transmigration of souls, since God, or the serpent *Da*, in accordance with the Platonic tradition, is primarily a geometrician.

In principle, the Voodoo vèvès are three astral planes that are the three "*pneumes*" of the African Cabala, being the three stages of the alchemic "*souffleurs*" or "prompters." These three astral planes are arranged in the diagram according to the magical attributes of the loas. This is the meaning given these planes by the tradition of the Great Solar Invisibles of Voodoo: (1) the invisible source of the stars; or the divine cosmos of omniscience, represented by the father or "*Plerome*," which is the idea of the preexisting light of the sun; (2) the visible stars whose light, coming from the Plerome is filtered by the moon or planetary cosmos of science, represented by the son or "*Paraclete*" which is the light of the sun; (3) the tangible objects, or physical cosmos of omnipotence of omniscience, represented by the mother as incarnate mystères (the loa " crisis") or "*Ophanim*."

In Voodoo, the father is "Omnipotent" or "*Até-Gbi-Ni-M-On-Sé*, as "Inexpressible" (the fire-air serpent); the son is the "Knowing One" or *Lé-Gba Ati-Gbon*, as "Expression of the Inexpressible Invisible" (snake-wood); the mother is the "Omniscient" or *Ai-Da Hwé-Do*, as "Concretion of the Inexpressible Grand Invisible" (earth-eater serpent).

The three astral planes correspond to a serpent-synthesis which is *ophitomorphic* or *ophitopentamorphic*, that is to say, which unites together as a macrocosm, all the elements of the microcosm or "human being." Thus it is that as serpent (*ophi-*) and mystère (*os* or *so*) with five heads (pentamorphic) these planes correspond to the five degrees of the Loa:

SOD.........................Mystères or Loas
THO-RAH..............Letter (of the Loa)
MI-CH-NA-as..........Spirit (of the Loa)
THA-EL-MUD........Ritual (of the Loa)
GUE-MA-RAH.......Complement (of the Loa)

These are the universal similarities of what Voodoo calls vèvès: the *Ky-il-k-or*, which like the vèvè is a ritual diagram designed ceremonially by the Tibetans on the ground with colored powders; the *Man-Da-Lah* of the Hindus; the Persian, Arabian, Berber *Tha-pi* or *Tapis*, upon which the faithful squats or kneels in order to arise towards the Invisibles; the magic buckler of the Aztecs and Toltecs; the *Ora-I-Bi Po-Wa-Nu* of the Precolumbian Indian rituals; the Chinese *Lit* or *Lih*; and the sand paintings of the American Indians. The vèvè, like its parallels, is a geometric, propitiatory support of planetary origin, and at the same time a condenser of astral forces designed to lead on the sacrificial victims.

Every time the celebrant prepares to trace a vèvè he should say, after orienting the material to be used in making the diagram, "By the power of the Loa LETE-MAGIE, Nègre Danhomé, all the vèvès, Nègre Bhacoulou Thi-Kaka."

From *Scarne's New Complete Guide to Gambling* by John Scarne (New York: Simon and Schuster, copyright © 1961, 1974 by John Scarne).

Scarne's New Complete Guide to Gambling

TYPES OF GAMBLERS

There are seven different kinds of men and woman gamblers. Which category are you in?

1. *The occasional gambler* who knows little or nothing about the hard mathematical and psychological facts of the games on which he now and then wagers some money. The vast majority of America's gamblers fall into this class, and it is their losses which make gambling our biggest industry.

2. *The degenerate or habitual gambler* who plays constantly and who knows considerably more about gambling but is not smart enough to know that he can't beat adverse odds. He craves action, any kind of action, and he lives in a dream world in which he hopes someday to make a big killing and then gambling forever. When he does win a bit, he almost always gambles it all back and, like most players, winds up broke.

3. *The skilled gambler or gambling hustler* who knows a lot more about any sort of gambling than the occasional or habitual gambler, plays a much better game than they do and consequently wins more often than he loses. He is usually on hand to start the game, and he specializes in games which contain some element of skill, such as Poker, Gin Rummy, Bridge or Black Jack. The hustler plays for blood: he seldom gives another player a break because he believes that is no way to earn money at gambling. He usually knows where the favorable percentage lies in most private games of chance, such as Craps, and he makes the most of this by offering the occasional and habitual gamblers sucker odds, which, not knowing any better, they usually accept.

4. *The professional gambler or gambling operator* who earns his living, or most of it, by operating some gambling scheme. He is called a gambler because he runs a gambling operation, but he doesn't really gamble. He is a businessman (or woman) who runs a gambling operation and understands his trade, and either makes direct levies on the play or receives a percentage because the odds are in his favor. The professional gambler, like the legitimate banker and insurance operator, acts as a middleman in risks which the players voluntarily take or wish to be rid of, charging a commission for the service. He is not betting against the players; they are actually betting against each other. His top aids are also in this category.

5. *The gambling cheat or crook* who makes money by cheating at cards or dice, running a fake lottery or raffle, operating a fixed carnival game, punchboard, slot machine or any other gaffed (crooked) gambling device. Also included in this category are any employees of a crooked gambling house or any participants in crooked schemes, whether or not they do the actual cheating themselves. The cheat's gamble is not so much in winning or losing as in whether or not he will get away with it.

6. *The gambling chiseler* who is really only a petty crook and sneak thief. He knows that he needs an edge to make money by gambling, and he gets it by inducing a friend at a racetrack or casino game to give or loan him money with which to gamble. He actually bets only part of the money and pockets the rest, and if he wins, he conceals all or part of the winnings. This is a favorite racket of women chiselers.

In a Poker game the chiseler often forgets to put up his ante at his turn of play, and he is quick to grab any sleeper (money belonging to another player which the latter has forgotten about). He will borrow money during a private game and forget about paying it back.

The chiseler—and there are millions of these characters—preys mostly on the habitual, chronic gambler. He is often caught, but that doesn't deter him, since he considers it an occupational hazard.

7. *The system gambler* who lives in a dream world all his own, believing that it is only a question of time until he finds an infallible betting system which he can use to amass a fortune. He is a perfect mark (sucker) for racetrack touts. He buys tips and most of the advertised systems, and although they fail, one after another, he buys more, always hoping to find the one that is perfect. The system horse player usually spends as much money on worthless tips and systems as he bets on the horses, and he wastes many hours trying to figure out a system of his own.

From *Allegory and the Migration of Symbols* by Rudolf Wittkower (New York: Thames and Hudson Inc., 1987). © 1977 Margot Wittkower.

Allegory and the Migration of Symbols

INTERPRETATION OF VISUAL SYMBOLS

...Representational meaning can not be understood unless the objects or events shown by the artist belong to the general human experience of the percipient. The latter must, moreover, have the obvious or hidden key to the represented concept in its totality, and he must be conversant, above all, with changing conventional idioms.

If all these requirements are fulfilled, we are still far from knowing the subject matter or theme. Representational meaning and the theme of a work rarely coincide. This happened only during brief periods of the history of art, in Europe for instance when artists began to paint pure landscape and still-life, i.e. when trees only mean trees and pots and apples only pots and apples. The rule may be exemplified with the 11th-century illumination in Plate 227. Correctly described on the representational level, it shows a figure with wings walking across the sea and handling a round object. Now, 'figure with wings' is an ambiguous symbol. It may signify as diverse concepts as Poetry, Virtue, Fame, Genius, Peace, Piety, history, and so forth. But if we are equipped with sufficient biblical and hagiographical knowledge (which in this case we acquired in childhood), we know that wings and halo supplement each other to signify 'angel'. For people outside the Christian tradition the intellectual concept 'angel', and therefore also its visual equivalent, remains unintelligible.

Like the artist we must know the conventional 'language' of attributes; we must know that 'bearded nude man with trident' means Neptune; or 'nude woman on ball' Fortuna. But this knowledge, though indispensable, is not sufficient. Full thematic interpretation requires information about the idea which assembled allegories express, or about the scenes which mythological figures enact. For this information we are dependent on a text or a verbal tradition. The visual message of the 11th-century illumination cannot be understood without the text from Revelation: 'and a mighty Angel took up a stone like a great millstone, and cast it into the Sea.' However, once we have learned the visual thematic convention for a specific story, its meaning will be revealed to us in the act of perception...

...On the level of representational meaning great numbers of people are capable of objective interpretations. Taking into account some limiting factors, relatively little experience is needed to 'read' correctly representational conventions at different historical moments, from prehistorical to modern art. The circle of those able to interpret the theme is considerably narrower. This depends first on a familiarity with the religious, mythological, literary, and social conditions of the civilization to which the work belongs, and secondly on the particular knowledge of the verbal or textual tradition which the work illustrates. The circle of the initiated narrows further when we turn to the third category, multiple meaning: it is accessible only to a relatively small and often very small minority of contemporaries and to the scholar who carefully scrutinizes the past and builds up his evidence, stone by stone. Finally, interpretative rather than descriptive analyses of the expressive function and meaning of line, form and colour in a given context are hardly capable of being tested objectively.

As we proceed from representational to thematic and on to multiple meaning and expression, it becomes more and more difficult to control the objectivity of statements. And the more we try to unravel in depth the meaning of a symbol, the more complex is the approach, and the greater the margin of misinterpretation.

It is hardly necessary to emphasize that the differentiation between four levels of meaning is, as is the case with every dissection of unified mental processes, of limited heuristic value. In actual fact, the 'what' can only be perceived through the 'how', and the inscrutable 'how' is thus the primary factor. Art can therefore not dispense with form, but it can dispense with the objective theme, as modern art often does. Nor is an objective theme necessary to express multiple meaning. But this is all the more open to misinterpretation when an intended subjective symbolism is interwoven with the intrinsic subconscious symbolism. And who can say where intended symbolism ends and subconscious symbolism begins? It is modern abstract art that has exposed this problem in all its complexity.

Biography

1964	Born in London
1982	Boston University, Boston
1983–1986	Camberwell School of Art, London, BFA
	Lives and works in New York City

ONE-PERSON EXHIBITIONS & EXHIBITION BIBLIOGRAPHY

1995

Working Model, Basilico Fine Arts, New York, February 18–March 18.

Drolet, Owen. "Matthew Ritchie at Basilico Fine Arts." *Flash Art*, Summer 1995, p. 129.

Kalina, Richard. "Matthew Ritchie at Basilico Fine Arts." *Art in America*, July 1995, p. 85.

Levin, Kim. "Voice Listings: Recommended: Matthew Ritchie." *The Village Voice*, March 7, 1995, p. 8.

Servetar, Stuart. "Matthew Ritchie at Basilico Fine Arts." *NY Press*, March 1, 1995, p. 49.

Smith, Roberta. "Matthew Ritchie at Basilico Fine Arts." *The New York Times*, March 10, 1995, p. C20.

1996

The Hard Way, Chapter I, Galerie Météo, Paris, September 14–October 19. Artist's Book, with essay by Nicolas Bourriaud (English and French), text by Matthew Ritchie, published by Galerie Météo, Paris.

Marguerin, Mathieu. "Matthew Ritchie: The Hard Way." *Blocnotes*, January–February 1997, pp. 120–121.

The Hard Way, Chapter II, Basilico Fine Arts, New York, October 19–November 23.

Bayliss, Sarah. "The Informers." *World Art*, no. 13, 1997, pp. 66–68.

Berman, Jennifer. "Matthew Ritchie." *Bomb*, Spring 1997, pp. 60–65.

Cotter, Holland. "Matthew Ritchie 'The Hard Way.'" *The New York Times*, November 15, 1996, p. C21.

Drolet, Owen. "Matthew Ritchie at Basilico Fine Arts." *Flash Art*, Summer 1996, p. 129.

Heartney, Eleanor. Review. *Art in America*, April 1997, p. 114.

Joo, Michael. "The Hard Way." *Performing Arts Journal*, September 1999, pp. 77–79.

Levin, Kim. "Voice Listings: Recommended." *The Village Voice*, November 12, 1996.

Melrod, George. Review. *Art & Antiques*, November 1996, p. 28.

Rubbini, Alice. Review. *Juliet Art Magazine*, no. 80, December 1996–January 1997, p. 58.

Saltz, Jerry. "The Hard Way." *Time Out New York*, November 7–14, 1996, p. 40.

Schaffner, Ingrid. "Matthew Ritchie." *Artforum*, March, 1996, p. 93.

The Hard Way, Chapter III, c/o Atle Gerhardsen, Oslo, December 14–January 28, 1997.

Blom, Ina. Review. *Aftenposten*, December 30, 1996, p. 13.

Kastner, Jeffrey. "The Weather of Chance: Matthew Ritchie and the Butterfly Effect." *Art/Text*, May–July, 1997, p. 54.

1997

Omniverse, Nexus Contemporary Art Center, Atlanta, November 1–December 20.

Cullum, Jerry. "Matthew Ritchie: Omniverse." *The Atlanta Journal-Constitution*, November 28, 1997, p. Q7.

1998

The Gamblers, Galeria Camargo Vilaça, São Paulo, March 3–March 28. Traveled to Paco Imperial, Rio de Janeiro, and Fundação Cultural de Distrito Federal, Brasília.

"Mostra questionam formas de percepção." *Folda de São Paulo*, March 3, 1998.

"Trabalhos que vão alem do estetico." *Jornal de Tarde*, March 1998, p. 8C.

The Gamblers, Basilico Fine Arts, New York, October 23–November 28. Artist's Book with essay by Helen Molesworth, text by Matthew Ritchie, published by Basilico Fine Arts, New York.

Levin, Kim. "Matthew Ritchie." *The Village Voice*, November 24, 1998, p. 76.

"Matthew Ritchie." *The New Yorker*, November 23, 1998, p. 18.

McDonough, Tom. "Matthew Ritchie at Basilico Fine Arts." *Art in America*, May 1999, p. 159.

Pinchbeck, Daniel. "New York Artist Q & A: Matthew Ritchie." *The Art Newspaper*, no. 86, November 1998, p. 71.

Smith, Roberta. "Matthew Ritchie." *The New York Times*, November 13, 1998, p. E40.

Yablonsky, Linda. "Matthew Ritchie, The Gamblers." *Time Out New York*, November 26–December 3, 1998, p. 63.

The Gamblers, Mario Diacono Gallery, Boston, November 21–January 20, 1999. Brochure with text by Mario Diacono.

1999

The Big Story, Cleveland Center for Contemporary Art, Cleveland, February 12–May 2. Artist's book with essay by Kristin Chambers text by Matthew Ritchie, published by Cleveland Center for Contemporary Art.

Litt, Steven. "Telling the Big Story." *The Plain Dealer*, February 28, 1999, pp. 1H–5H.

The Working Group, c/o Atle Gerhardsen, Baloise Art Preis, Art Statement, Basel Art Fair, Basel, Switzerland, June 14–June 21. Traveled to c/o Atle Gerhardsen, Oslo, August 19–September 25.

Dobrzynski, Judith. "In Olympics of Art World, Anything for an Edge." *The New York Times*, June 17, 1999, pp. C1–C4.

Sandberg, Lotte. "Explosivt Ekspanderende Maleri." *Aftenposten*, August 26, 1999, p. 28.

2000

The Fast Set, Museum of Contemporary Art, North Miami, March 31–June 25. Artist's book with essays by Bonnie Clearwater, text by Matthew Ritchie, published by the Museum of Contemporary Art, North Miami.

Moshkovitz, Boris. "Ritchie at MoCA." *Flash Art*, May–June 2000, p. 55.

Wilson-Goldie, Kaelen. "Matthew Ritchie's Matrix: An Artist Re-creates the World in Seven Steps." *Black Book*, Summer, 2000, pp. 56–58.

Parents and Children, Andrea Rosen Gallery, New York, October 21–November 25.

Cotter, Holland. "Matthew Ritchie." *The New York Times*, November 24, 2000, p. E36.

Ellis, Patricia. "Matthew Ritchie: That Sweet Voodoo You Do." *Flash Art*, November–December 2000, pp. 88–91.

Gilmore, Jonathan. "Matthew Ritchie: Andrea Rosen." *Tema Celeste*, January/February 2001, p. 94.

Hunt, David. "When Worlds Collide." *Time Out New York*, November 16–23, 2000, p. 81.

Kastner, Jeffrey. "An Adventurer's Map to a World of Information." *The New York Times*, October 15, 2000, p. AR37.

Jones, Ronald. "Matthew Ritchie." *Frieze*, no. 58, 2001, pp. 101–102.

Saltz, Jerry. "Out There." *The Village Voice*, November 28, 2000, p. 79.

Schwabsky, Barry. "Matthew Ritchie: Andrea Rosen Gallery." *Artforum*, January 2001, p. 137.

Concentrations 38: Matthew Ritchie, Dallas Museum of Art, Dallas, January 25–April 21. Artist's book, *The Slow Tide*, with essay by Suzanne Weaver, text by Matthew Ritchie, published by the Dallas Museum of Art.

Kutner, Janet. "Particle Poetics." *The Dallas Morning News*, March 7, 2001, p. 5C.

McCabe, Bret. "The Slow Tide." *Glass Tire*, www.glasstire.com.

The Family Farm, White Cube, London, October 19–November 24.

Buck, Louisa. "Matthew Ritchie." *The Newspaper International Edition*, October 2001, p. 74.

Coomer, Martin. "Matthew Ritchie." *Time Out London*, November 20, 2001, p. 63.

de Cruz, Gemma. "Matthew Ritchie." *Art Review*, October 2001, pp. 64–67.

2002

After Lives, Andrea Rosen Gallery, New York, October 19–November 23.

Richard, Frances. "Matthew Ritchie: Andrea Rosen Gallery." *Artforum*, January 2003, p. 136.

Smith, Roberta. "Cracking the Same Mold with Different Results." *The New York Times*, November 14, 2002, p. E38.

2003

After the Father Costume, c/o Atle Gerhardsen, Berlin, April 25–May 31.

Pulfer, Reto, and Christophe Wiesner. "Matthew Ritchie: After the Father Costume." *Neue Review—Art in Berlin*, no. 2, July 2003, p. 11.

Stange, Reimer. "Augen wie Billardkugeln." *Der Tagesspiegel*, May 2003, p. 28.

GROUP EXHIBITIONS

1990

David McCaig & Matthew Ritchie, Judy Nielsen Gallery, Chicago.

1991

Blood, JAARY, Finland.

1992

9 x 2, Artists Space, New York.

1993

Back Room, Natalie Rivera, New York.

Inconsequent, Natalie Rivera, New York.

New York, San Juan & Toronto, Leonora Vega Gallery, San Juan, Puerto Rico.

1994

Matthew Ritchie & Nestor Otero, Leonora Vega Gallery, San Juan, Puerto Rico.

Grey, Grodesky, Judd, Ritchie, Smithson, Mitchell Algus Gallery, New York, April 23–May 28.

The Circumscribed Imagination on the Ruins of Tradition, Mario Diacono Gallery, Boston, September 17–October 28.

modus operandi, Leonora Vega Gallery, New York.

1995

Ten + Ten, New York Studio School, New York, January 5–February 18.

Möbius Strip, Basilico Fine Arts, New York, January 7–February 11. Catalogue with texts by Liam Gillick and Matthew Ritchie.

Color: Sign, System, Sensibility, Stark Gallery, New York, June 6–July 21.

Summer Fling, Basilico Fine Arts, New York, June 6–July 28.

Verrückt, Schloss Agathenburg, Agathenburg, Germany, September 24–November 26. Traveled to Museum der Stadt, Arolsen, Germany, April–May 1996. Catalogue with essays by Joachim Buttler and Nasim Weiler, et al.

Anecdote by Juxtaposition #1, Livet Reichard Co., New York.

A Vital Matrix, domestic setting gallery, Los Angeles. Catalogue.

1996

Between the Acts, Ice Box, Athens, January 17 – February 29. Catalogue with essay by Devon Dikeou.

New Work: Drawings Today, San Francisco Museum of Modern Art, San Francisco, January 17 – June 3.

Screen, Friedrich Petzel Gallery, New York, January 19 – February 24.

Between the Acts, c/o Atle Gerhardsen, Oslo, April 13 – April 23.

Architecture/Application/Complication, Room, New York, April 27 – May 25.

AbFab, Feature, New York, May 17 – June 22.

A Scattering Matrix, Richard Heller Gallery, Santa Monica, California, November 16 – December 14.
Catalogue with essay by Jane Hart.

Adicere Animos, La Galleria d'Arte Moderna e Contemporanea e Pinacoteca Nazionale, Cesena, Italy.
Catalogue with essay by Alice Rubbini.

1997

The Body of Painting, Mario Diacono Gallery, Boston, January 18 – March 1.

météo-show, Galerie Météo , Paris, May 20 – July 30. Catalogue.

1997 Biennial, Whitney Museum of American Art, New York, March 20 – June 15. Catalogue with essays
by Louise Neri and Lisa Phillips.

In-form, Bravin Post Lee, New York, June 4 – July 19.

Project Painting, Basilico Fine Arts and Lehmann Maupin, New York, September 10 – October 11.
Catalogue with essay by Ingrid Schaffner.

Art on Paper, Weatherspoon Art Gallery, The University of North Carolina at Greensboro,
November 16, 1997 – January 18, 1998. Catalogue with introduction by Amy Capellazzo.

Map the Gap, storefront for Art & Architecture, New York.

Objectif Lune, CAN Centre d'Art Neuchatel, Neuchatel, Switzerland.

1998

Art Today, Indianapolis Museum of Art, Indianapolis, February 19 – March 8.

Parallel Worlds, South East Center for Contemporary Art, Winston-Salem, North Carolina, April 25 – July 5.
Brochure with essay by Ron Platt.

Exploiting the Abstract, Feigen Contemporary, New York, May 2 – June 13.

Codex USA, Entwistle Gallery, London, June 4 – August 1.

Deep Thought, Basilico Fine Arts, New York, June 11 – July 31.

Painting: Now and Forever, Part I, Matthew Marks Gallery and Pat Hearn Gallery, New York, June 26 – July 31.

More Fake, More Real, Yet Ever Closer, Castle Art Gallery, College of New Rochelle, New Rochelle,
New York, November 8, 1988 – January 15, 1999. Catalogue with essay by Robert Evren.

Hindsight – Recent Acquisitions and Gifts from the Permanent Collection, Whitney Museum of American
Art, New York, December 17, 1998 – January 21, 1999.

Transatlantico, Centro Atlantico de Arte Moderno, Canary Islands, Spain.

1999

Drawn by…, Metro Pictures, New York, January 23 – February 20.

Continued Investigation of the Relevance of Abstraction, Andrea Rosen Gallery, New York, January 29 –
February 27.

Conceptual Art: A Neurobiological Praxis, Thread Waxing Space, New York.

Story, A/C Project Room, New York, September 9 – October 9.

Cyber Cypher, Mario Diacono Gallery, Boston, September 18 – December 19.

Best of the Season, Aldrich Museum of Contemporary Art, Ridgefield, Connecticut, September 26, 1999 –
January 9, 2000.

Mondo Immaginario – projektionen und pigmente, Schendhalle, Zurich, October 1 – November 28.

2000

Faith, The Aldrich Contemporary Art Museum, Ridgefield, Connecticut, January 23 – May 29. Catalogue
with essay by Harry Philbrick.

Unnatural Science, Mass MoCA, North Adams, Massachusetts, May 1, 2000 – May 15, 2001. Catalogue
with essays by John Ackerman and Laura Steward Heon.

Drawing Spaces, Rhona Hoffman Gallery, Chicago, May 3 – May 31. Catalogue.

Vision Machine, Musée des Beaux-Arts de Nantes, Nantes, France, May 12 – September 10. Catalogue
with essay by Ariel Pelenc.

Drawings 2000, Barbara Gladstone Gallery, New York, July – August. Catalogue with essay by
Klaus Kertess.

Museum, Astrup Fearnley Museet for Moderne Kunst, Oslo, June 15 – September 24. Catalogue.

Celebrating Modern Art: The Anderson Collection, San Francisco Museum of Modern Art, San Francisco,
October 7, 2000 – January 15, 2001. Catalogue with essay by Neil Benezra.

Hypermental: Rampant Reality 1950 – 2000 from Salvador Dali to Jeff Koons, Kunsthaus Zurich, Zurich,
Switzerland, November 17, 2000 – January 21, 2001. Catalogue with essays by Christof Heinrich
and Bice Curiger. Traveled to Hamburger Kunsthalle, February 16 – May 6, 2001.

2001

Pictures, Patents, Monkeys, and More…On Collecting, Western Gallery, Western Washington University,
Bellingham, Washington, January 9 – March 10. Catalogue with essay by Ingrid Schaffner. Traveled
to John Michael Kohler Arts Center, Sheboygan, Wisconsin, August 12 – October 21; Akron Art
Museum, Akron, Ohio, November 17 – February 24, 2002; Fuller Museum of Art, Brockton,
Massachusetts, June 1 – August 18, 2002; Institute of Contemporary Art, University of Pennsylvania,
Philadelphia, September 15 – November 10, 2002; and Pittsburgh Center for the Arts, Pittsburgh,
January 18 – March 16, 2003.

All Systems Go, Contemporary Arts Museum Houston, Houston, January 11 – March 4. Catalogue with essay by Lynn M. Herbert.

New Acquisitions from the Dakis Joannou Collection, Centre for Contemporary Art, Athens, February 9 – May 26.

The World According to the Newest and Most Exact Observations: Mapping Art and Science, The Tang Teaching Museum and Art Gallery, Skidmore College, Saratoga Springs, New York, March 3 – June 3. Catalogue with essays by Ian Barry and Susan Bender.

010101: Art in Technological Times, San Francisco Museum of Modern Art, San Francisco, March 3 – July 8, Catalogue with essays by Benjamin Weil, et al.

Collaborations with Parkett: 1984 – Now, The Museum of Modern Art, New York, April 5 – June 5. Catalogue.

Selections from the Permanent Collection, Museum of Contemporary Art, North Miami, June 1 – September 21.

futureland2001.com, Museum Van Bommel-Van Dam, Venlo, The Netherlands, September 9 – December 2; and Städtisches Museum Abteiberg, Mönchengladbach, Germany, September 24, 2001 – January 6, 2002. Catalogue with essay by Veit Loers.

The Mystery of Painting, Sammlung Goetz, Munich, October 29, 2001 – April 5, 2002. Catalogue with essays by Rainald Schumacher, et al.

Form Follows Fiction, Castello di Rivoli, Torino, Italy, October 15, 2001 – January 27, 2002. Catalogue with essay by Jeffrey Deitch.

2002

Flights of Reality, Kettle's Yard, University of Cambridge, Cambridge, England, January 12 – March 3. Catalogue essay by Simon Groom. Traveled to The Turnpike Gallery, Greater Manchester, England, April 20 – June 8.

Urgent Painting, LARC/Musée d'Art Moderne, Paris, January 15 – March 3. Catalogue with essays by Patricia Falguieres, Caroline Jones, and Matthew Ritchie.

Virginie Barré + Christophe Berdaguer & Marie Péjus + Alain Declercq + Michael Elmgreen & Ingar Dragset + Naomi Fisher + Gelatin + Subodh Gupta + Alexander Györfi + Kay Hassan + Gunilla Klingberg + Surasi Kusolwong + Michel Majerus + Paola Pivi + Matthew Ritchie + Franck Scurti + Wang-Du +Sislej Xhafa + Jun'ya Yamaide, Palais de Tokyo, Paris, January 21 – April 21.

Sprawl, The Contemporary Arts Center, Cincinnati, March 24 – June 20.

(The World May Be) Fantastic, Biennale of Sydney of 2002, Sydney, May 15 – July 14. Catalogue with essay by Richard Grayson and text by Matthew Ritchie.

Reverberator, Houldsworth Gallery, London, May 30 – July 6.

Drawing Now: Eight Propositions, Museum of Modern Art, Queens, New York, October 16, 2002 – January 7, 2003. Catalogue with essay by Laura Hoptman.

Once Upon a Time, New York State Museum, Albany, New York, December 14 – March 9, 2003.

2003

Painting Pictures, Kunstmuseum Wolfsburg, Wolfsburg, Germany, March 1 – June 29. Catalogue with essay by Annelle Lutgens.

Journey to Now, Art Gallery of South Australia, John Kaldor Art Projects and Collection, Adelaide, Australia, April 18 – July 6.

GNS (Global Navigation System), Palais de Tokyo, Paris, June 5 – September 7. Catalogue with essay by Nicolas Bourriaud.

Hands Up, Baby, Hands Up! 160 Jahre Oldenburger Kunstverein, 160 Arbeiten auf Papier, Oldenburger Kunstverein, Oldenburg, Germany, September 12 – October 26. Catalogue.

ARTIST'S PROJECTS

PERMANENT INSTALLATIONS

Games of Chance and Skill (2002). Albert and Barrie Zesiger Sports and Fitness Center, Massachusetts
Institute of Technology, Cambridge, Massachusetts.
The Deep Six (2002). Shiodome City Center, Tokyo.

WEB PROJECTS

The Hard Way (1996). Walker Art Center, Minneapolis.
http://adaweb.walkerart.org/influx/hardway/
The New Place (2001). San Francisco Museum of Modern Art, San Francisco.
www.sfmoma.org/010101
Games of Chance and Skill (2002). Massachusetts Institute of Technology, Cambridge, Massachusetts.
http://web.mit.edu/matthew-ritchie

CURATORIAL PROJECTS

The Ruined Map. Curated by Matthew Ritchie, *zing magazine*, Autumn 1996
(available at http://www.zingmagazine.com/zing3/index.html).
DEMONCLOWNMONKEY. Curated by Matthew Ritchie, Artists Space, New York, March 21–May 11, 2002.

CRITICAL WRITINGS

"The Anatomy of Redemption." *Segno*, January–February 1994, pp. 52–55.
"The Architecture of Possibility." *Performing Arts Journal*, no. 54, September 1996, pp. 53–57.
"Carroll Dunham: Sonnabend." *Flash Art International*, May–June 1995, pp. 113–114.
"Dark Matters." *Carroll Dunham: Paintings.* New York: The New Museum of Contemporary Art and Hatje
Cantz, 2002, pp. 86–108.
"Dietrich Orth." *Flash Art International*, November–December 1994, p. 96.
"The Edge of Love: The Transformation of Forrest Bess." *Fat Magazine*, Winter 1995/96, pp. 8–9.
"Gabriel Orozco." *Flash Art International*, January–February 1995, p. 96.
"hot.list." *Artforum*, May 1999, p. 27.
"Itai Doron." *Flash Art International*, October 1995, p. 108.
"In Three Parts: Liam Gillick." *Performing Art Journal*, no, 53, 1996, pp. 68–71.
"Katy Schimert." *Bomb*, Winter 1998, pp. 89–90.
"Lisa Yuskavage: Marianne Boesky." *Flash Art International*, March–April 1997, p. 119.
"Lorna Simpson: Sean Kelly Gallery." *Flash Art International*, March–April 1996, p.112.
"Love, Sweat, and Tears." *Flash Art International*, November–December 1997, pp. 78–80.
"Matthew Barney's Cremaster 5." *Flash Art International*, January–February 1998, pp. 108–109.
"Michael Joaquin Grey." *Public Offerings.* Los Angeles: Los Angeles Museum of Contemporary Art, 2001

"Michael Joaquin Grey: Five of a Kind." *art/text*, no. 58, August–October 1997, pp. 52–57.
"Michael Joo, Imagine." *Flash Art International*, November–December 1994, pp. 69–70.
"Michael Rees." *Flash Art International*, March–April 1995, p. 108.
"The New City." *art/text*, May–July 1999, pp. 74–79.
"People in Glass Houses: Laurie Simmons." *frieze*, no. 57, 2001, pp. 62–63.
"Richard Misrach: Curt Marcus." *Flash Art International*, Summer 1995, p. 127.
"Rosemarie Trockel." *Flash Art International*, January–February 1995, p. 95.
"Rules of Engagement: William Anastasi." *William Anastasi* (Orkney: Pier Arts Centre, 1995).
"Shaping a New Environment." *Flash Art International*, Anniversary Issue 1998, p. 100.
"Spotlight: Matthew Barney." *Flash Art International*, October 1995, p. 105.
"The Third Sex." *Flash Art International*, January–February 1995, pp. 51–52.
"Tony Cragg." *Flash Art International*, May–June 1994, p. 113.
"Tony Oursler: Technology as an Instinct Amplifier." *Flash Art International*, January–February 1996,
pp. 76–79.
"The Untold Story: Bonnie Collura." *Performing Arts Journal*, no. 58, January 1998, pp. 87–90.
"Video Spaces: Eight Installations at MoMA." *zing magazine*, no. 1, Autumn 1995.
"The World Made Flesh." *Flash Art International*, May–June 1995, pp. 71–72.
"Xavier Veilhan." *zing magazine*, no. 1, Autumn 1995.

BIBLIOGRAPHY

ARTIST'S BOOKS AND PROJECTS

The Hard Way. Paris, France: Galerie Météo, 1996. Essay by Nicolas Bourriaud and text by Matthew Ritchie.

The Gamblers. New York: Basilico Fine Arts, 1998. Essay by Helen Molesworth and text by Matthew Ritchie.

The Big Story. Cleveland, Ohio: Cleveland Center for Contemporary Art, Ohio, 1999. Essay by Kristen Chambers and text by Matthew Ritchie.

The Fast Set: Incomplete Projects 01. Miami: Museum of Contemporary Art, North Miami, 2000. Essay by Bonnie Clearwater and text by Matthew Ritchie.

The Slow Tide: Incomplete Projects 02. Dallas: Dallas Museum of Art, Texas, 2001. Essay by Suzanne Weaver and text by Matthew Ritchie.

Sea State One: Incomplete Projects 03. New York: Artists Space, 2001.

The Bad Need: Incomplete Projects 04. New York: Parkett, 2001. Edition for *Parkett* 61. Text by Matthew Ritchie.

Games Of Chance and Skill: Incomplete Projects 05. Cambridge: Massachusetts Institute of Technology, 2002. Essay by Jenelle Porter and text by Matthew Ritchie.

The Father Costume. Sebastopol, California: Artspace Books, 2002. Text by Ben Marcus, drawings by Matthew Ritchie.

BOOKS, INTERVIEWS, AND ARTICLES

1994

Drolet, Owen. "Group Show at Mitchell Algus, New York." *Flash Art*, October 1994, p. 53.

Han, M.T. "Matthew Ritchie at Leonora Vega." *Flash Art*, Summer 1994, p. 139.

Lezama, Manuel. "Matthew Ritchie, Nestor Otero." *The San Juan Star*, April 27, 1994.

Rouette-Gomez, Enid. "Matthew Ritchie Continues Quest for Perfection." *The San Juan Star*, April 17, 1994.

Stapen, Nancy. "The Circumscribed Imagination on the Ruins of Tradition." *The Boston Globe*, October 6, 1994.

1995

Brockmann, Adolph. "Videos com Stillen Ortchen." *Hamburger Abendblatt*, September 25, 1995, p. 31.

Kock, Mechthild. "Verrückt: Aggrissiv bis leichtfüssig." *Stader Tageblatt*, September 25, 1995.

Schiff, Hajo. "New York im Schloss." *Taz Hamburg*, September 27, 1995, p. 23.

1996

Dikeou, Devon. "Destruction has its own Beauty." *Eyilon*, February 25, 1996.

Princenthal. Nancy. "Artist's Book Beat." *On Paper*, vol. 1, no. 1, September – October, 1996.

Servetar, Stuart. "Masters and Notable Seconds." *Artnet*, October, 1996.

Tsingou, Emily, and Devon Dikeou, "Do the Right Thing." *The Art Magazine*, no. 24, 1996, p. 78.

Konst Varlden, Stockholm, no. 2, May – June, 1996, p. 70.

1997

Bayliss, Sarah. "Blake's Progress." *On Paper*, vol. 1, no. 5, May – June, 1997, pp. 24 – 27.

Marcoci, Roxana. *Art Now.* New York: Henry N. Abrams, 1997, p. 108.

1998

Brown, Cecily. "Painting Epiphany: Happy Days Are Where, Again?" *Flash Art*, May/June, 1998, pp. 76 – 79.

Fox, Catherine. "Mixing It Up in Style." *The Atlanta Journal Constitution*, August 21, 1998.

Relyea, Lane. "Virtually Formal." *Artforum*, September 1998, pp. 126 – 33.

"Matthew Ritchie." *L'Uomo Vogue*, September 1998, pp. 296 – 99.

1999

Gerster, Ulrich. "Rückzugsmodelle." *Neue Zürcher Zeitung*, October 29, 1999, p. 46.

Jones, Ronald. "Continued Investigation of the Relevance of Abstraction." *Frieze*, June/July/August 1999, pp. 102 – 103.

Kandel, Susan. "Matthew Ritchie," *Cream.* New York and London: Phaidon Press, 1999, pp. 348 – 51.

Smith, Roberta. "Continued Investigation of the Relevance of Abstraction." *The New York Times*, February 12, 1999, p. E39.

Smith, Roberta. "Galleries Are Labs of a Sort." *The New York Times*, February 14, 1999, p. AR39.

Zimmer, William. "7 Artists Integrate Color and Rudeness." *The New York Times*, January 10, 1999.

Zimmermann, Mark. "Colloquial Arabesques." *PAJ*, May, 1999, vol. 21, no. 62, pp. 72 – 75.

2000

Hofmann, Isabelle. "Die Geburt der Zeit." *Hamburger Morgenpost*, May 17, 2000.

Kane, Mitchell, Matthew Ritchie, Peter Lunenfeld, and Michael Joaquin Grey. "User – An Operating Criteria." in *Plan): A Working Meeting to Develop a Hybrid Product*, Northbrook, Illinois: Hirsch Foundation, 2000.

Kato, Emiko. "Matthew Ritchie." *Studio Voice*, vol. 297, September 2000, p. 33.

Glueck, Grace. "Creative Souls Who Keep the Faith or Challenge Its Influence." *The New York Times*, May 2000.

Levin, Kim. "Masters of the Universe." *The Village Voice*, May 22, 2000, p. 125.

Mack, Gerald. "Big Bang in Farbe." *CASH*, no. 21, May 26, 2000, p. 85.

Sheets, Hilarie. "Baffled, Bewildered and Smitten." *Art News*, September 2000, pp. 130 – 34.

Sischy, Ingrid. "Gotta Paint!" *Vanity Fair*, February 2000, pp. 140–47.
"Kunsthalle freut sich uber Wunschkind aus Basel." *Hamburger Abendblatt*, May 17, 2000.
"Mapping the Millennium." *The New York Times Magazine*, September 16, 2000, pp. 100–101.

2001
Bourbon, Matthew. "Gambling 'Over Seven Pays Even.'" *NYArts*, March 2001.
Galison, Peter, and Caroline Jones. "Theories and the Dead." *Parkett*, no. 61, 2001, pp. 148–53.
Marcus, Ben. "The Least You Need to Know About Radio." *Parkett*, no. 61, 2001, pp. 162–69.
Nakamura, Marie-Pierre. "Matthew Ritchie." *art actuel*, January–February 2001, pp. 70–73.
Nugent, Benjamin. "Innovators. Time 100: The New Wave." *Time*, October 15, 2001, p. 91.
O'Connor, John. "Diagramming Preference." *ArtistSpectrum*, volume 10, 2001, pp. 5–9.
Princenthal, Nancy. "The Laws of Pandemonium." *Art in America*, May 2001, pp. 144–49.
Rabinowitz, Cay Sophie. "Not Two, Not Three, Not Even Four Dimensions." *Parkett*, no. 61, 2001, pp. 138–41.
American Visionaries: Selections from the Whitney Museum of American Art. New York: Harry N. Abrams,
    Inc., 2001.
"Art Program 2001." *Bomb*, Summer 2001, p. 13.

2002
Bradley, Alexandra. "Matthew Ritchie: The Family Farm," in *White Cube*. London: Steidl, 2002, pp. 22–23.
Chambers, Christopher. "Notes from the Dawn of Time." *D'Art*, vol. 5, no. 3, Fall 2002, p. 31.
Dunham, Carrol, and Scott Rothkopf. "Road Food." *Artforum*, November 2002, pp. 132–37.
Firstenberg, Lauri. "Painting Platform in NY." *Flash Art*, November–December 2002, pp. 70–75.
Gamwell, Lynn. *Exploring the Invisible: Art, Science, and the Spiritual*. Princeton and Oxford:
    Princeton University Press, 2002, pp. 290–91.
Harris, Jane. "Matthew Ritchie," *Vitamin P*. New York and London: Phaidon Press, 2002, p. 282–83.
Matthew Higgs. *Reality Check: Painting in the Exploded Field*. San Francisco: The California College
    of Arts and Crafts, 2002.
Kelley, Tina. "For Patients, Welcome Relief from 4 Bare Walls." *The New York Times*, May 17, 2002, p. B5.
Lloyd, Ann Wilson. "Art Is a Necessity Among Techies, Too." *The New York Times*, December 15, 2002,
    pp. AR 50–51.
Schjeldahl, Peter. "The Drawing Board." *The New Yorker*, November 4, 2002, pp. 102–3.

2003
Griffin, Tim. "80s Again." *Artforum*, April 2003, p. 78.
Wilson-Goldie, Kaelen. "The New Abstractionists." *Art + Auction*, July 2003, pp. 92–97.
Siegel, Katy. "Matthew Ritchie: Contemporary Arts Museum," *Artforum*, September, 2003, p. 81.

CONTEMPORARY ARTS MUSEUM HOUSTON

BOARD OF TRUSTEES

STAFF

JOSEPH R. ADAMS, JR.
EDWARD R. ALLEN, III
DR. BERNARD A. AROCHA
THOMAS AU
CAROL BALLARD
TONI BEAUCHAMP
THOMAS A. BRES
DEBORAH BROCHSTEIN
ELLIE ALLDAY CAMBERG
ROBERT J. CARD, MD
BOB CASEY, JR.
SYLVIA CAVAZOS
SUSIE CRINER
DON DEPASQUALE
G. STEPHEN FINLEY
DEBORAH FIORITO
DIEDRA B. FONTAINE
JOE FRENCH
WILLIAM J. GOLDBERG
LAINIE GORDON
JULIA L. GREER
PATRICIA A. GREGORY
JOHN F. GUESS, JR.
RACHEL HECKER
ISABELL SMITH HERZSTEIN
ELIZABETH HOWARD
ELAINE JEFFERSON
LOUISE JAMAIL CHAIR
LEONARD JONES
SISSY KEMPNER
J. DAVID KIRKLAND, JR.
CARMEN KNAPP
MIGUEL LOYA
ISABEL STUDE LUMMIS
LESTER MARKS
VIRGINIA MITHOFF
DESRYE MORGAN
RICHARD S. MORGAN
JUDY NYQUIST
ANNISE D. PARKER
KATHLEEN T. PRESSLER
KAREN PULASKI
HOWARD ROBINSON
DAVID I. SAPERSTEIN
JEFF SHANKMAN
REGINALD R. SMITH
SARA DODD SPICKELMIER
STEPHEN D. SUSMAN
BECCA CASON THRASH
LAURA MORRIS WALLS
MARCY TAUB WESSEL
BLAKE YOUNG
MICHAEL ZILKHA

LEIGH ANDREWS MEMBERSHIP MANAGER
TIM BARKLEY REGISTRAR
TAMIKA BEATTY GIFTS PROCESSING COORDINATOR
CHERYL BLISSITTE ADMINISTRATIVE ASSISTANT, DIRECTOR'S OFFICE
ROBERT BOWDEN FINANCE OFFICER
DIANE BULANOWSKI SECURITY SUPERVISOR
VALERIE CASSEL OLIVER ASSOCIATE CURATOR
CRISTINA DEBOBEN GRANTS AND GIFTS MANAGER
ELLEN EFSIC DIRECTOR OF DEVELOPMENT
KENYA F. EVANS ASSISTANT PREPARATOR
NATIVIDAD FLORES HOUSEKEEPER
PETER HANNON IT MANAGER/WEB MASTER
LYNN M. HERBERT SENIOR CURATOR
CARLOS LAMA EDUCATION ASSOCIATE
MARTI MAYO DIRECTOR
PAOLA MORSIANI CURATOR
PAULA NEWTON DIRECTOR OF EDUCATION AND PUBLIC PROGRAMS
PETER PRECOURT TEEN COUNCIL COORDINATOR/EDUCATION ASSOCIATE
SUE PRUDEN MUSEUM SHOP MANAGER
MICHAEL REED ASSISTANT DIRECTOR
TRAVIS RICE ASSISTANT SECURITY SUPERVISOR
JEFF SHORE HEAD PREPARATOR
LANA SULLIVAN RECEPTIONIST/STAFF SECRETARY
AMY TABOR MUSEUM SHOP ASSISTANT
KELLY WATSON EVENTS MANAGER

Artist's Acknowledgements

I worked on this project with many talented people and it certainly would not have been possible without their committment and insight. Thank you: Jordan Bastien, Sarah Cohen, Jim Caffrey, Teri Caffrey, Jessica Frost, Don Gratz, Atle Gerhardsen, Jon Lash, David Lasry, Lucy Minturn, Molly Lenore, Conny Purtill, Jenelle Porter, John Rannou, Andrea Rosen, Nick Roth, and Joey Stein.

Singular thanks are due to Karen Leo, whose humor, generosity and passion for life has made this and every other project we have worked on such a pleasure.

To Lynn Herbert and the entire staff at CAMH: thank you for the working experience of a lifetime. The installation crew at CAMH were exemplary, many thanks to: Tim Barkley, Rachel Cook, Jamal Cyrus, Paul Druecke, Kenya Evans, Jonathan Groom, Christopher Huron, Brian Moss, Robert Pruitt, Jeff Shore, Shelby Spaulding, Stephen Taylor and Hunter Wakefield.

The floor and heads were fabricated with generous support from The Fabric Workshop and Museum; special thanks to Marion Stroud, Doug Bohr, and the indefatigable Sue Patterson. The material for the floor was generously donated by Johnsonite. The heads were produced from decimated digital files based on heads originally made by Grace Dunham and by students at Wharton Elementary School, Houston, in collaboration with the artist. Thank you: Grace Dunham, Oscar Gonzalez, Brenda Gonzalez , Vinh Ngo, Jeremy King, Natalia Lopez, Denise Aguilar, Brandon Boyd, Tish Condado, Martin Milian, Nora Garcia and Doren Garcia, for your time and help. Special thanks to Karyn Olivier, artist & student instructor. Thanks also to Dr. Bob Sandburn, Executive Director, Education Foundation of Harris County and Monica Sandoval, Principal, Wharton Elementary School.

A portion of the game was made with assistance from the Eyebeam Moving Image Division.

This show is dedicated to my extraordinary wife and son.

FIG. 34: MATTHEW RITCHIE (RIGHT) AND KARYN OLIVIER (LEFT) WITH STUDENTS AT WHARTON ELEMENTARY SCHOOL, HOUSTON, WORKING ON HEADS FOR *THE FINE CONSTANT* (2003)

Published by the Contemporary Arts Museum Houston
in association with Hatje Cantz Publishers
Senefelderstaße 12
73760 Ostfildern-Ruit, Germany
T + 49 7 11 4 40 50
F + 49 7 11 4 40 52 20
www.hatjecantz.de

Distribution in the U.S.A.
Distributed Art Publishers, Inc. (D.A.P.)
155 Avenue of the Americas
New York, NY 10013-1507 USA
T 212 627 1999
F 212 627 9484
www.artbook.com

Publication coordinators: Lynn M. Herbert and Jenelle Porter
Editor: Polly Koch
Design: Purtill Family Business
Printed by Dr. Cantz'sche Druckerei, Ostfildern-Ruit

Copyright © 2003 Contemporary Arts Museum Houston and
Hatje Cantz Publishers, Ostfildern-Ruit
All rights reserved.
No part of this publication may be reproduced
without the written permission of the publisher.
Printed and bound in Germany.

Library of Congress Control Number: 2003098732
ISBN 0-936080-84-1 and 3-7757-9186-8

Contemporary Arts Museum Houston
5216 Montrose Boulevard
Houston, Texas 77006-8250
T 713 284 8250
F 713 284 8275
www.camh.org

Photography:
Art Resource, NY: fig. 6
Courtesy c/o Atle Gerhardsen, Berlin: pp. 88, 111, 115 (bottom right)
Jenni Carter: p. 91
Cathy Carver: fig. 2
Courtesy Contemporary Arts Museum Houston: figs. 8–27, 34; p. 48
Patrick Drickey: p. 87
Hester + Hardaway: fig. 1; pp. 2, 4, 5, 13–15, 20, 21, 26 (top left);
        49–54, 64
Penguin Books (USA) Inc.: fig. 3
Franco Maria Ricci Editore, Milan: fig. 4
Matthew Ritchie: pp. 26 (right and bottom), 27, 57–63
Courtesy Andrea Rosen Gallery, New York: figs. 28–31; pp. 28–37,
        65, 69, 70, 89, 92–95, 101–103, 107, 109, 113, 115 (top and
        bottom left), 116
Scala/Art Resource, NY: figs. 5, 7
Oren Slor: pp. 25, 66–68, 71–79, 90
White Cube, London: p. 104, 105

FOR THIS CATALOGUE, THE FOUR LETTERS USED TO DENOTE THE FOUR CONSTANTS OF THE UNIVERSE—e, h, G, AND c (THE ELECTRON CHARGE, THE PLANCK LIMIT, GRAVITY, AND THE SPEED OF LIGHT)—HAVE BEEN PRINTED IN
RED, GOLD, GREEN, AND BLUE RESPECTIVELY.
FRONT AND BACK COVER: *THE HIERARCHY PROBLEM* (DETAIL), 2003, ACRYLIC ON WALL, 12 x 139 FEET (3.6 x 42.3 M), COURTESY THE ARTIST AND ANDREA ROSEN GALLERY, NEW YORK